Save Mother Oil on Canvas   70.8"   × 51.1"   2008

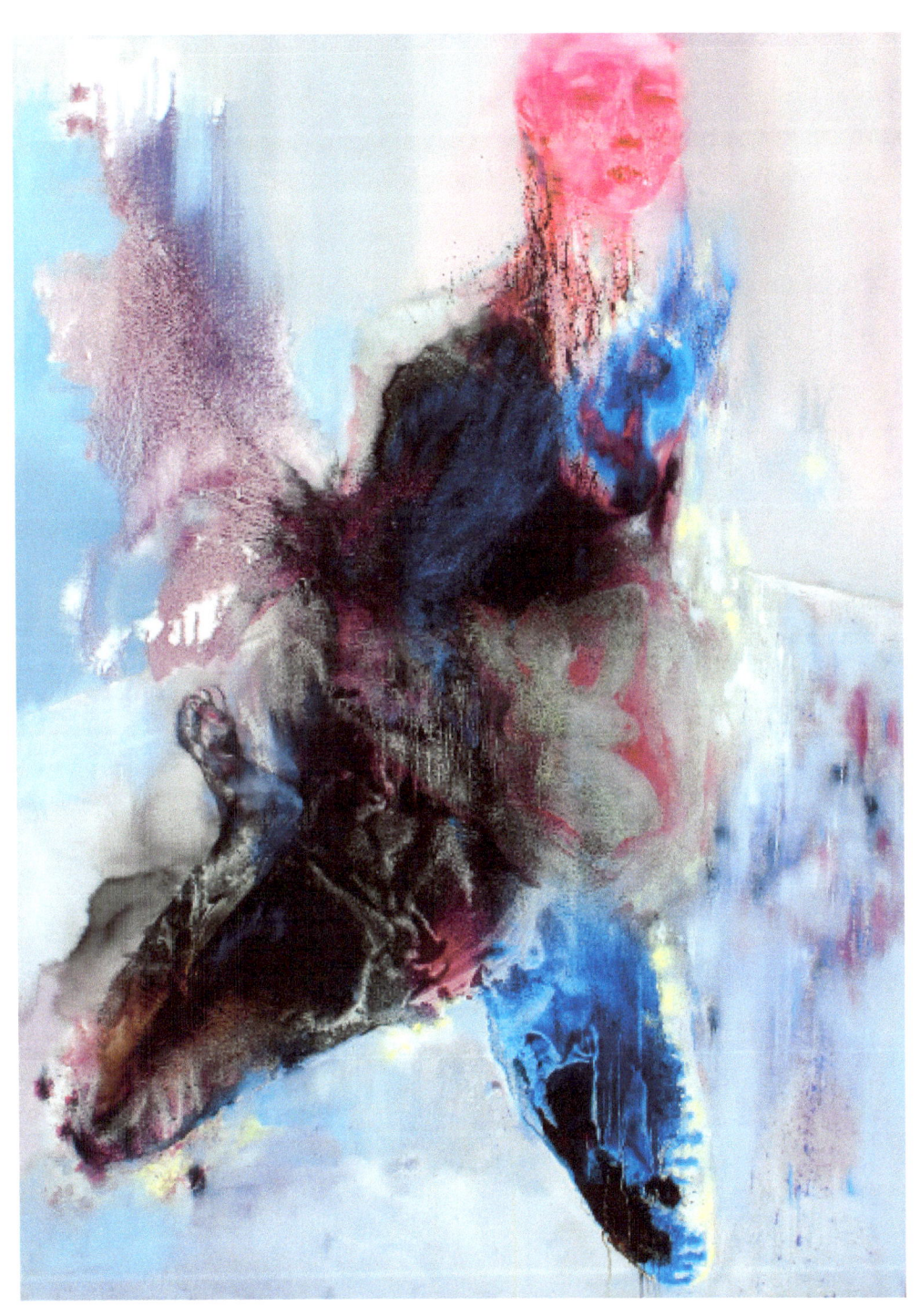

Please Forgive Me Oil on Canvas   70.8"   × 51.1"   2008

Fox's Love Oil on Canvas   47.2"   × 59"   2009

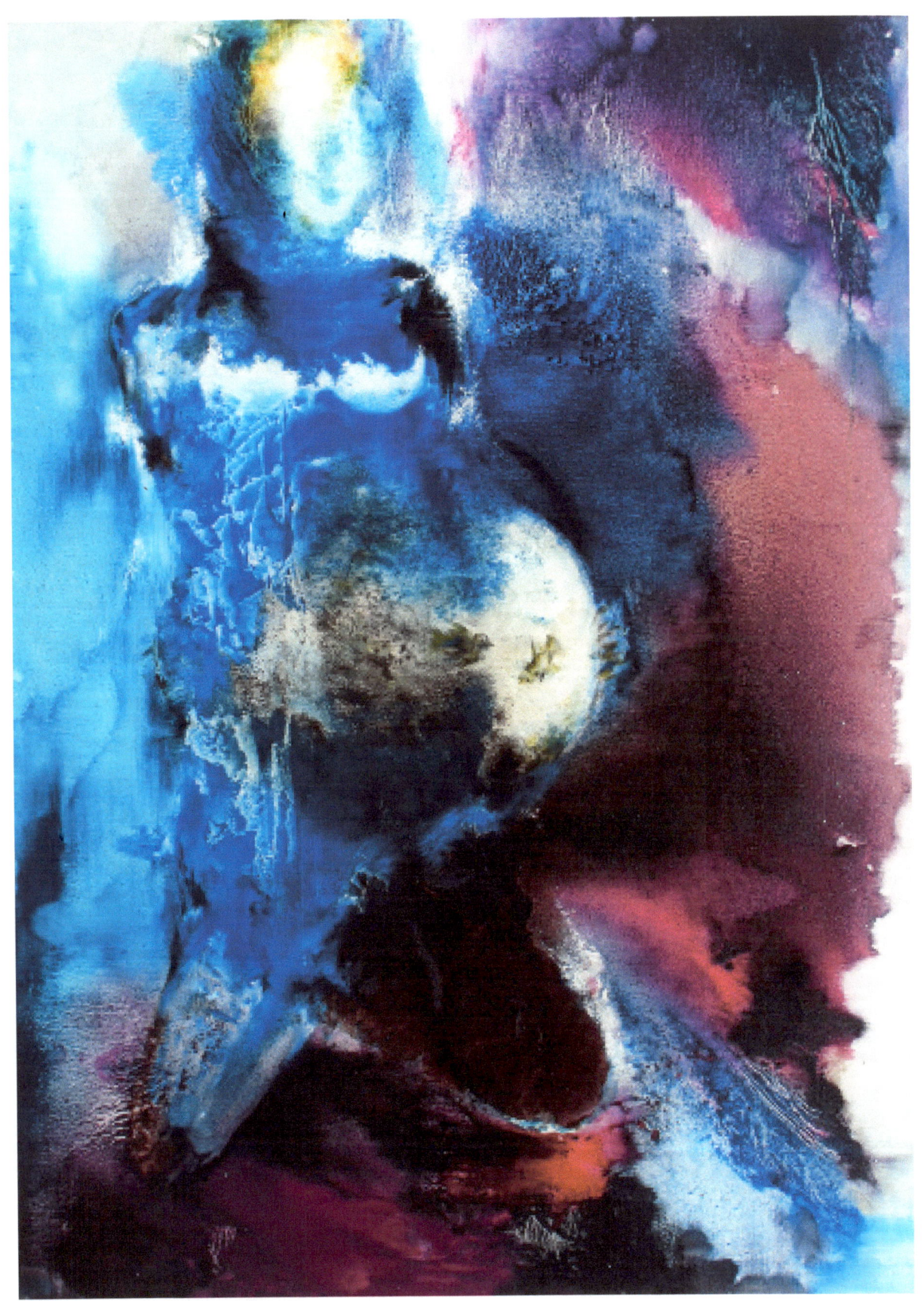

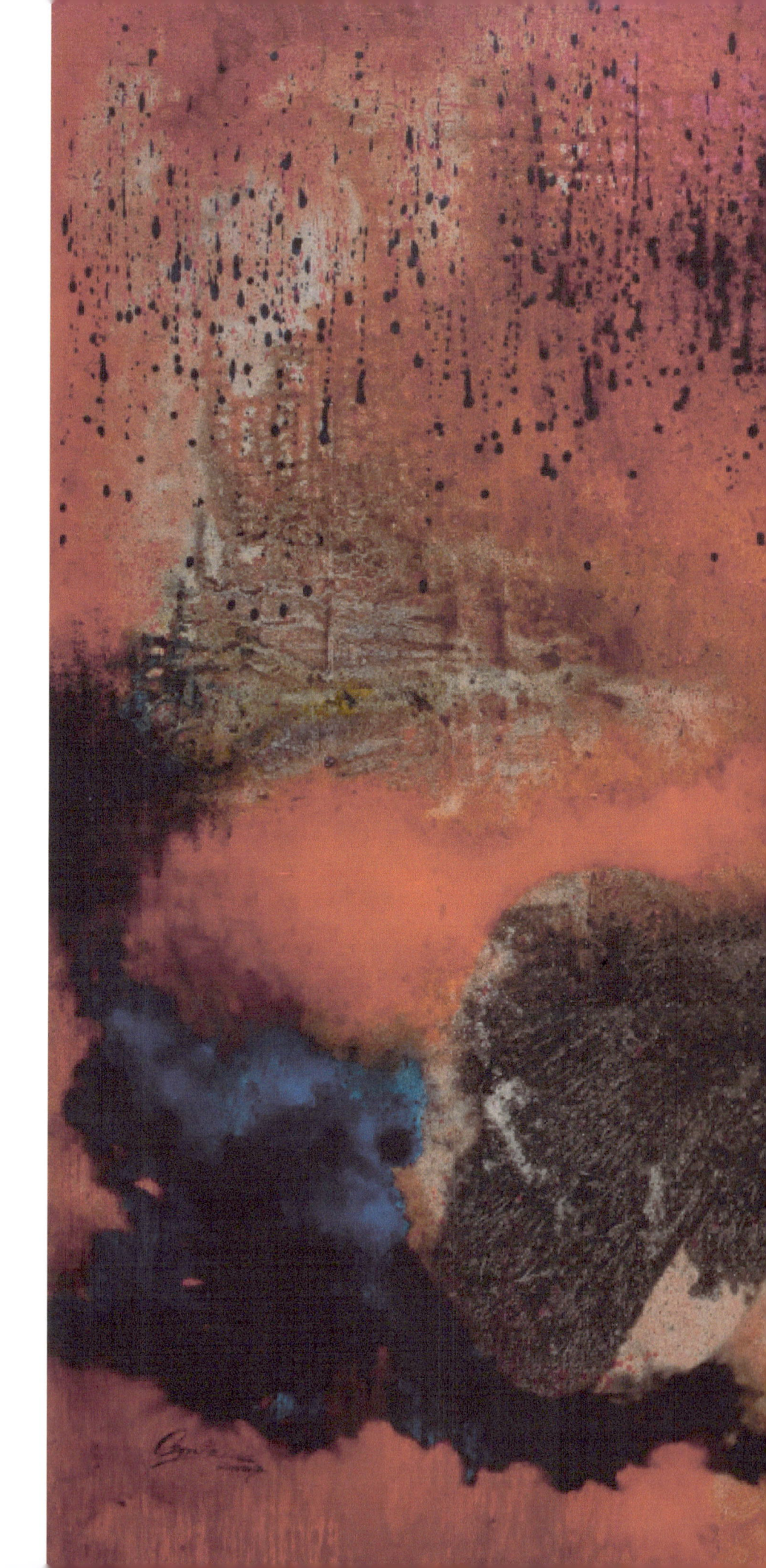

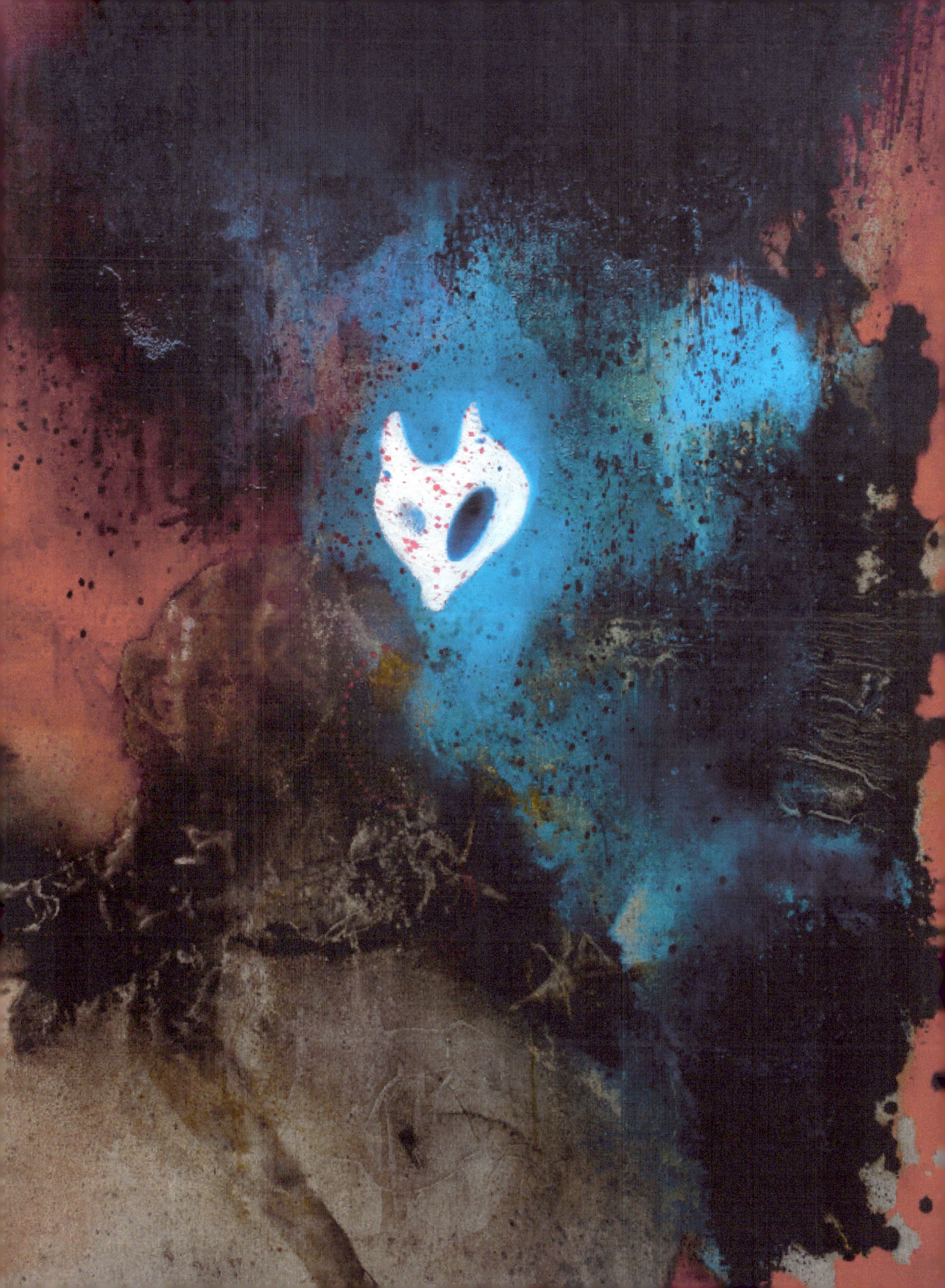

Temptation Oil on Canvas   35.4"   × 35.4"   2012

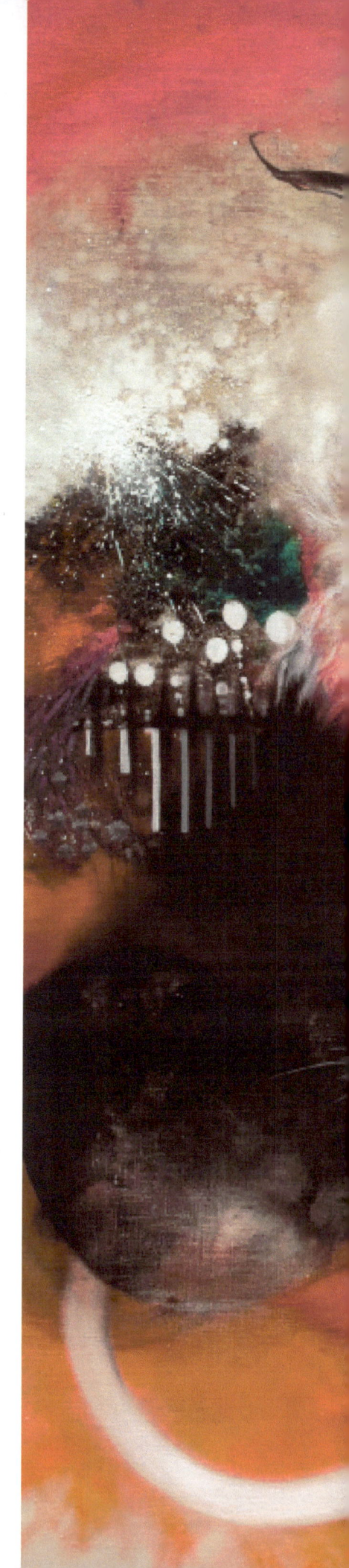

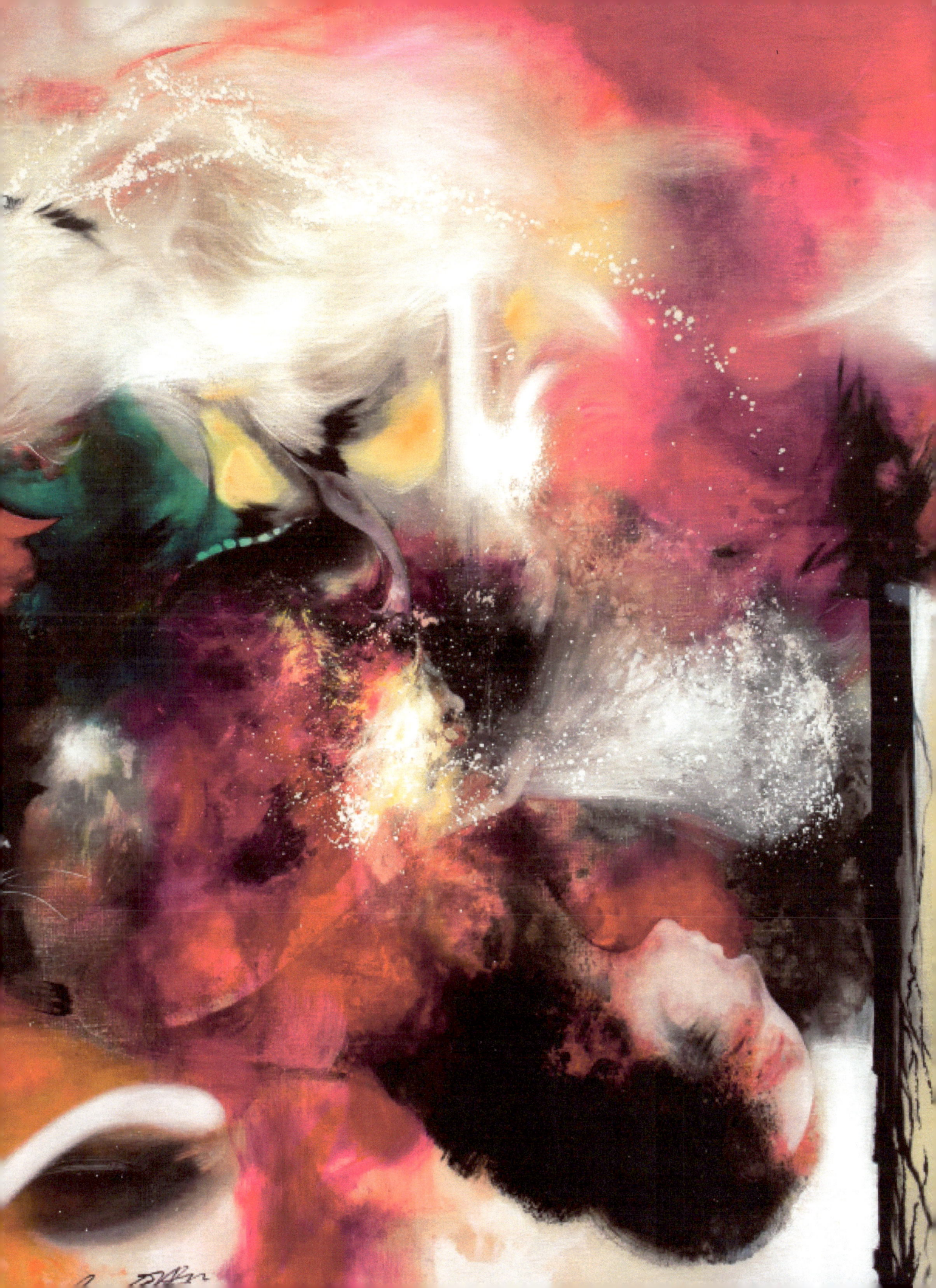

Dancing Shoes Oil on Canvas   31.5" × 15.7"   2009

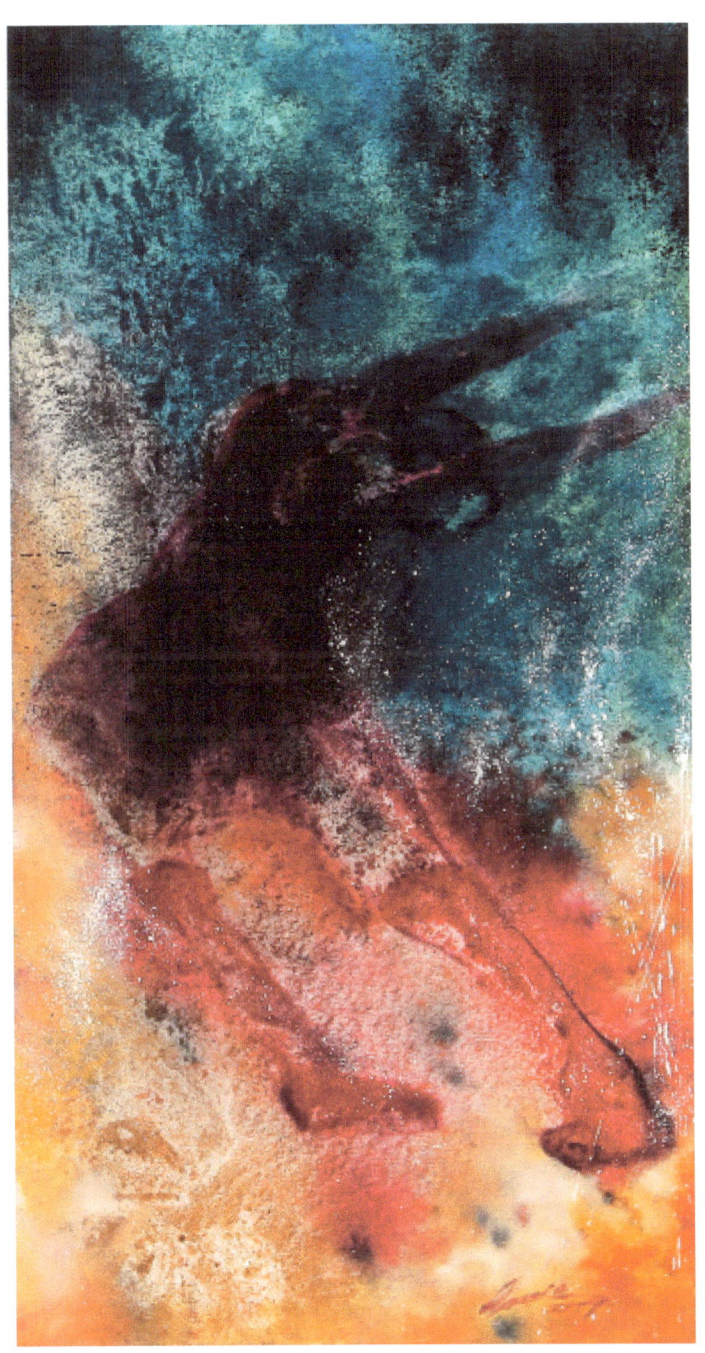

More Attractive than Makeup Oil on Canvas   31.5" φ 2012

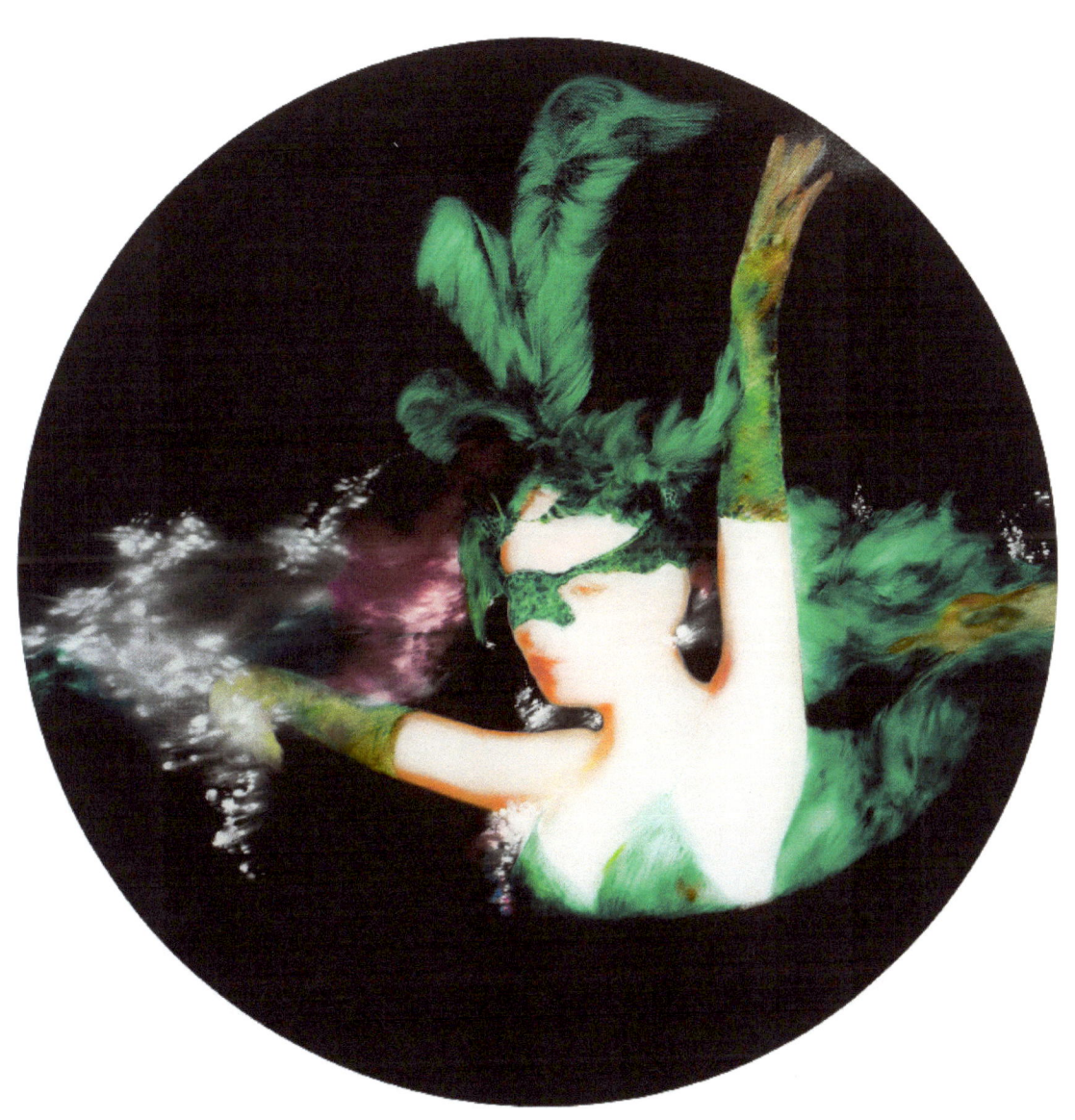

Maid Oil on Canvas   70.8”   × 51.1” 2009

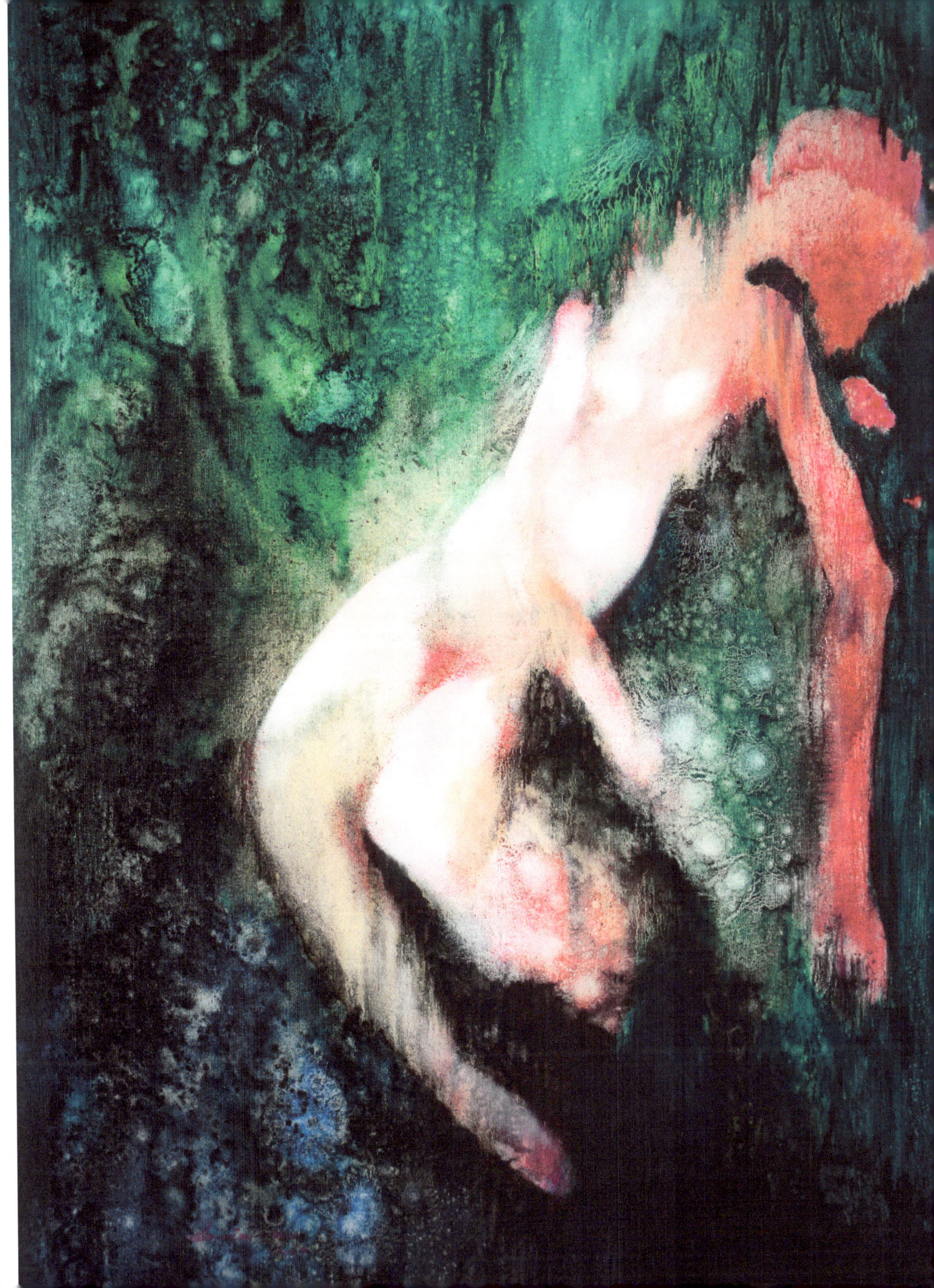

Hurt Oil on Canvas   70.8"   × 51.1"   2009

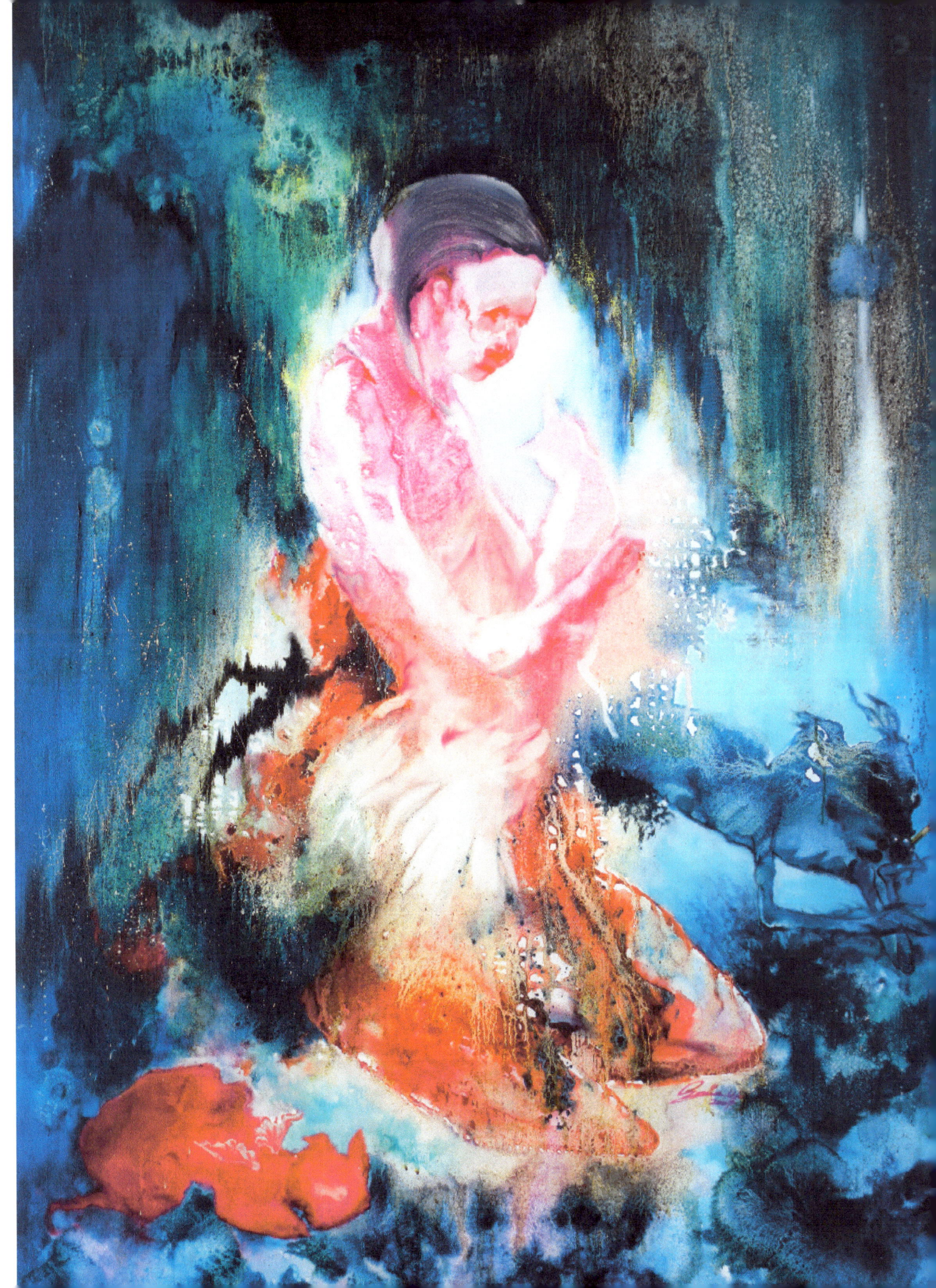

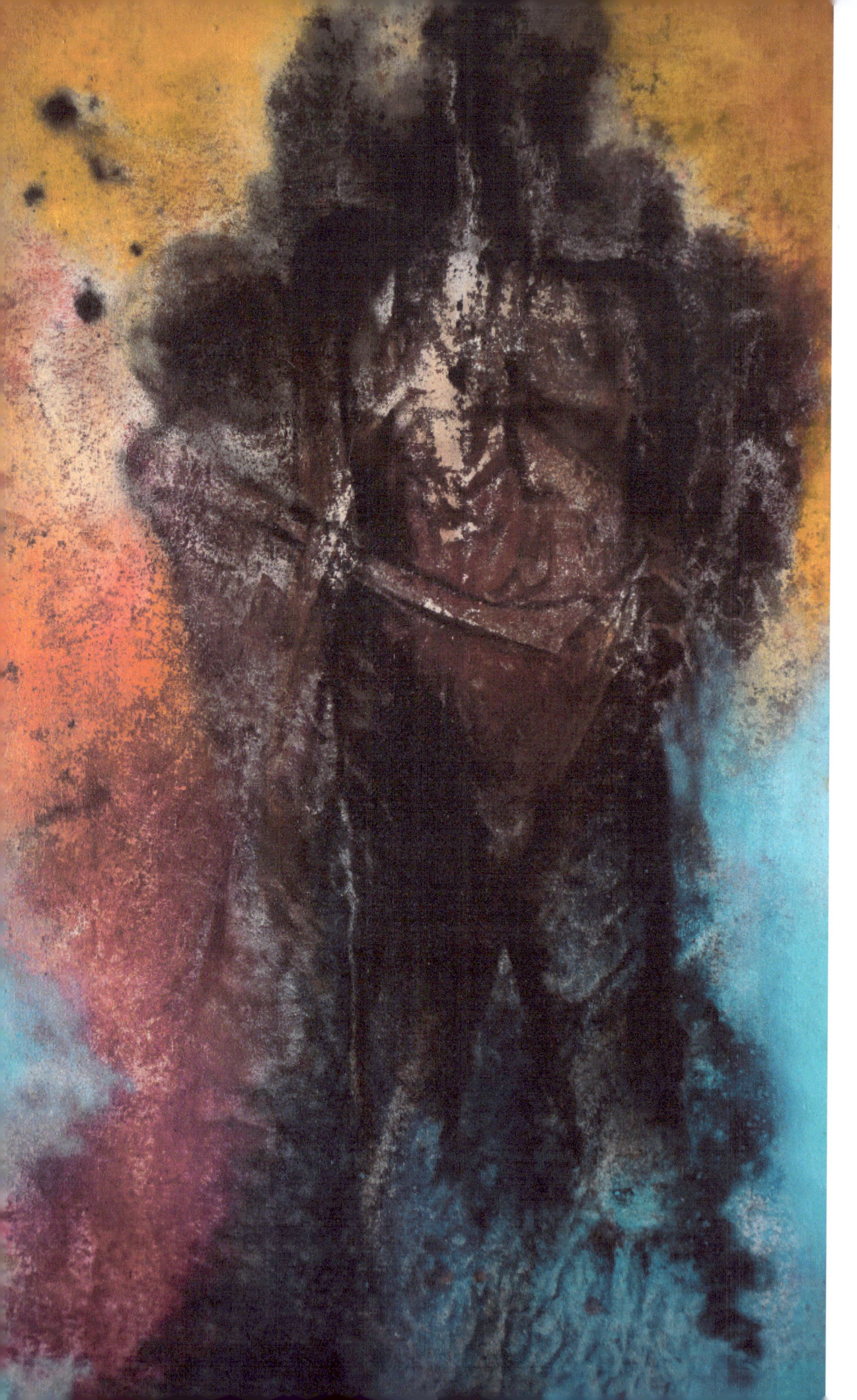

Perplexed Oil on Canvas 39.3" × 23.6" 2009

Kids Oil on Canvas   70.8"   × 51.1"   2008

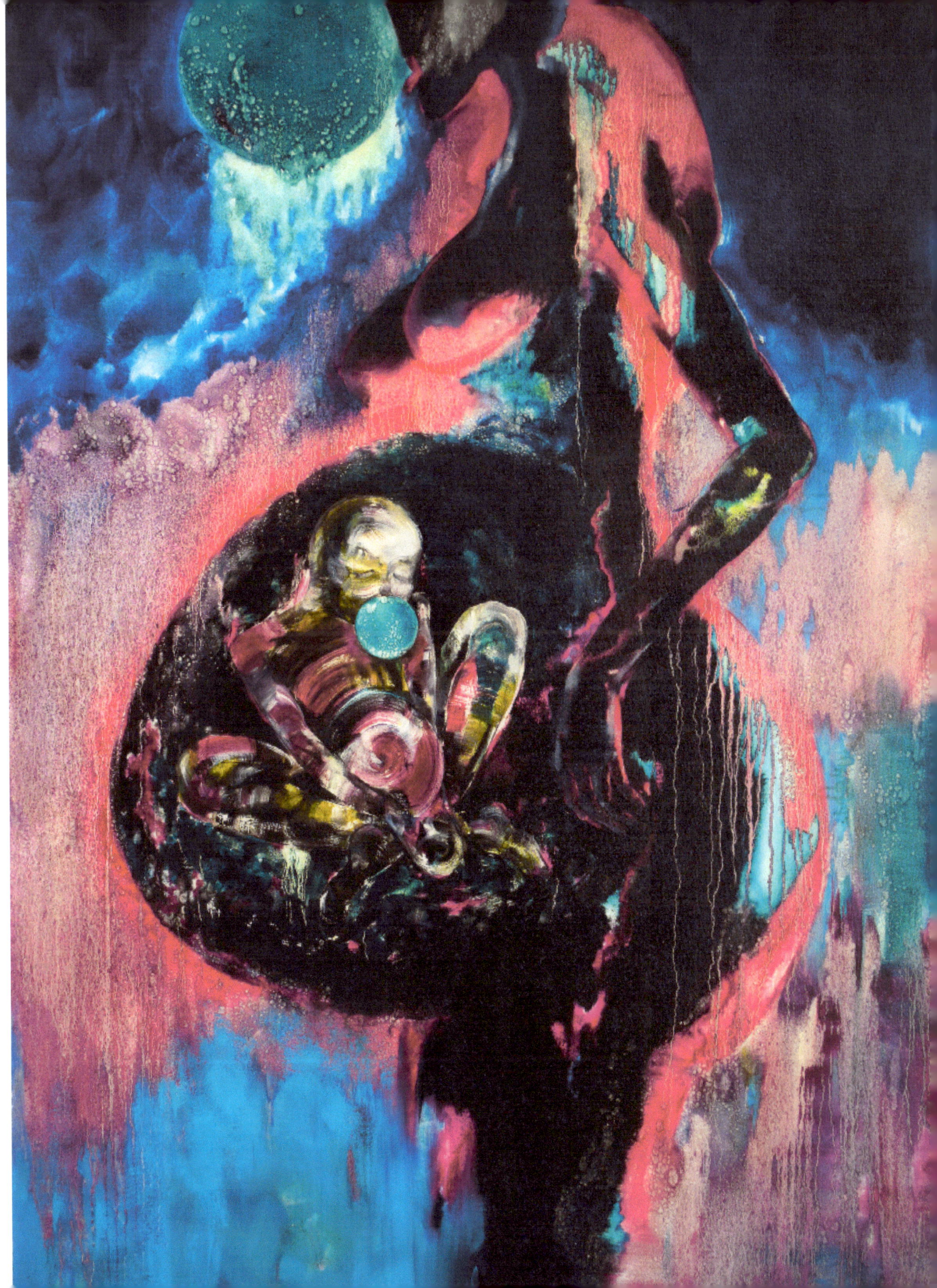

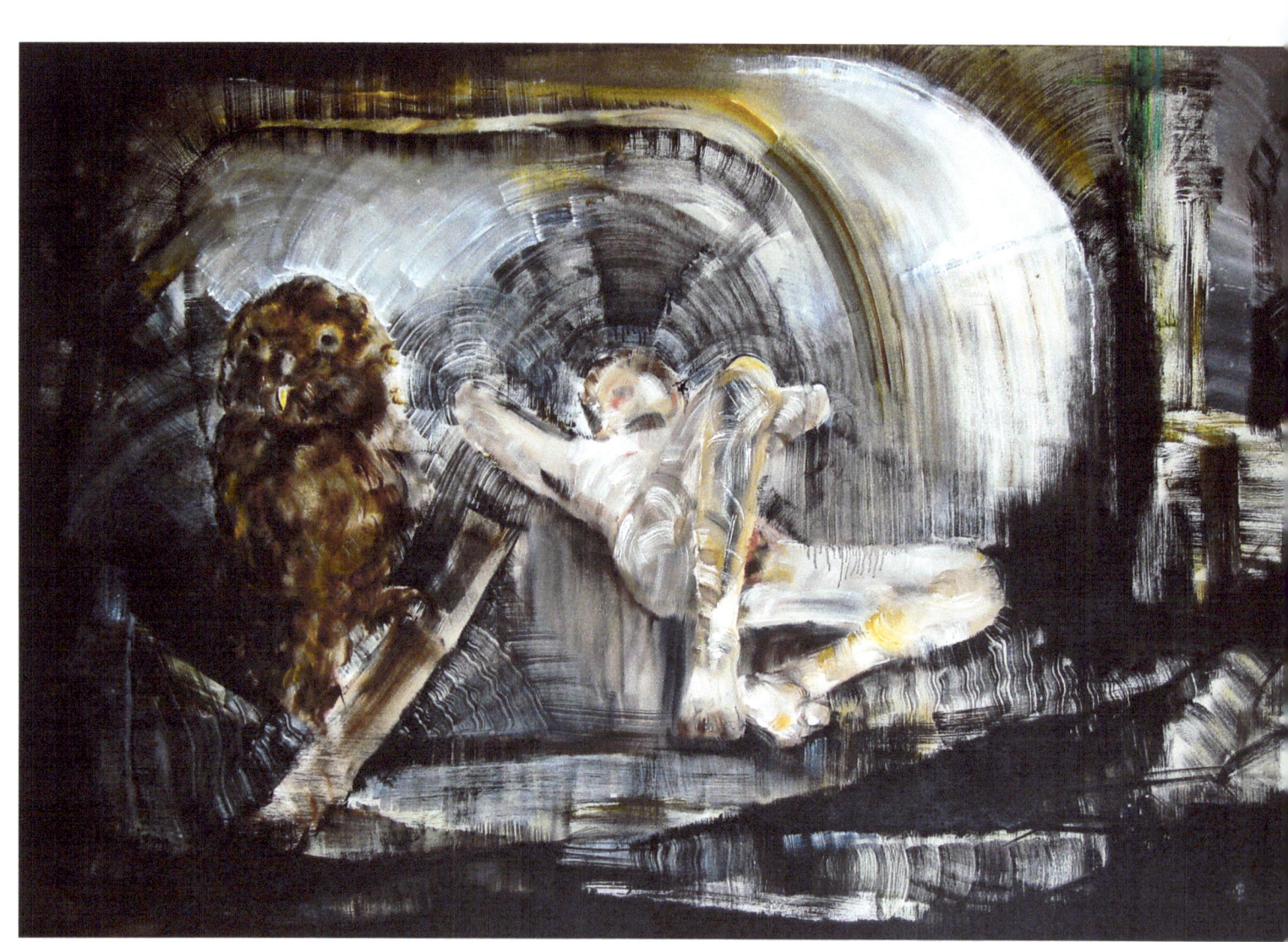

Untitled Oil on Canvas 39.3" × 55.1" 2008

Wildlife Oil on Canvas   39.3"   × 39.3"   2013

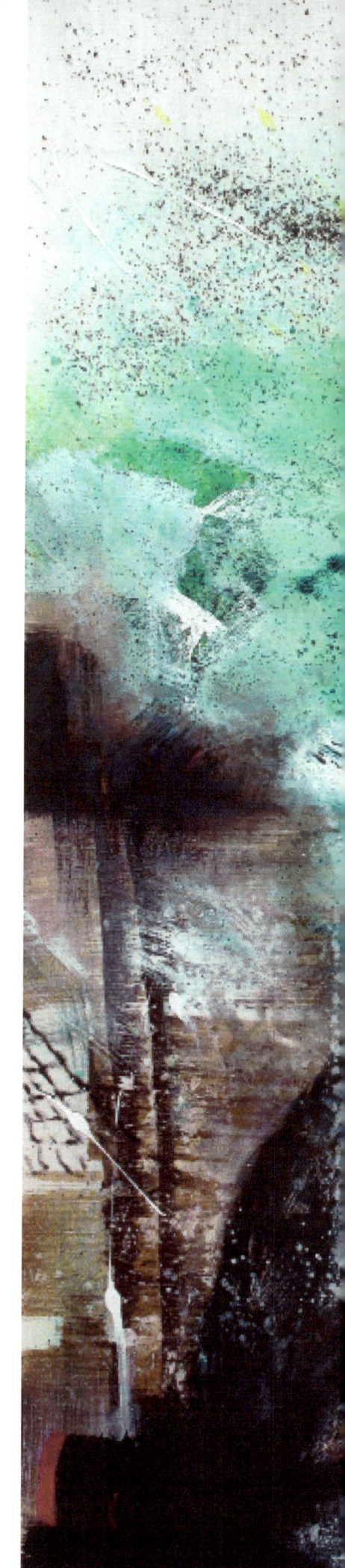

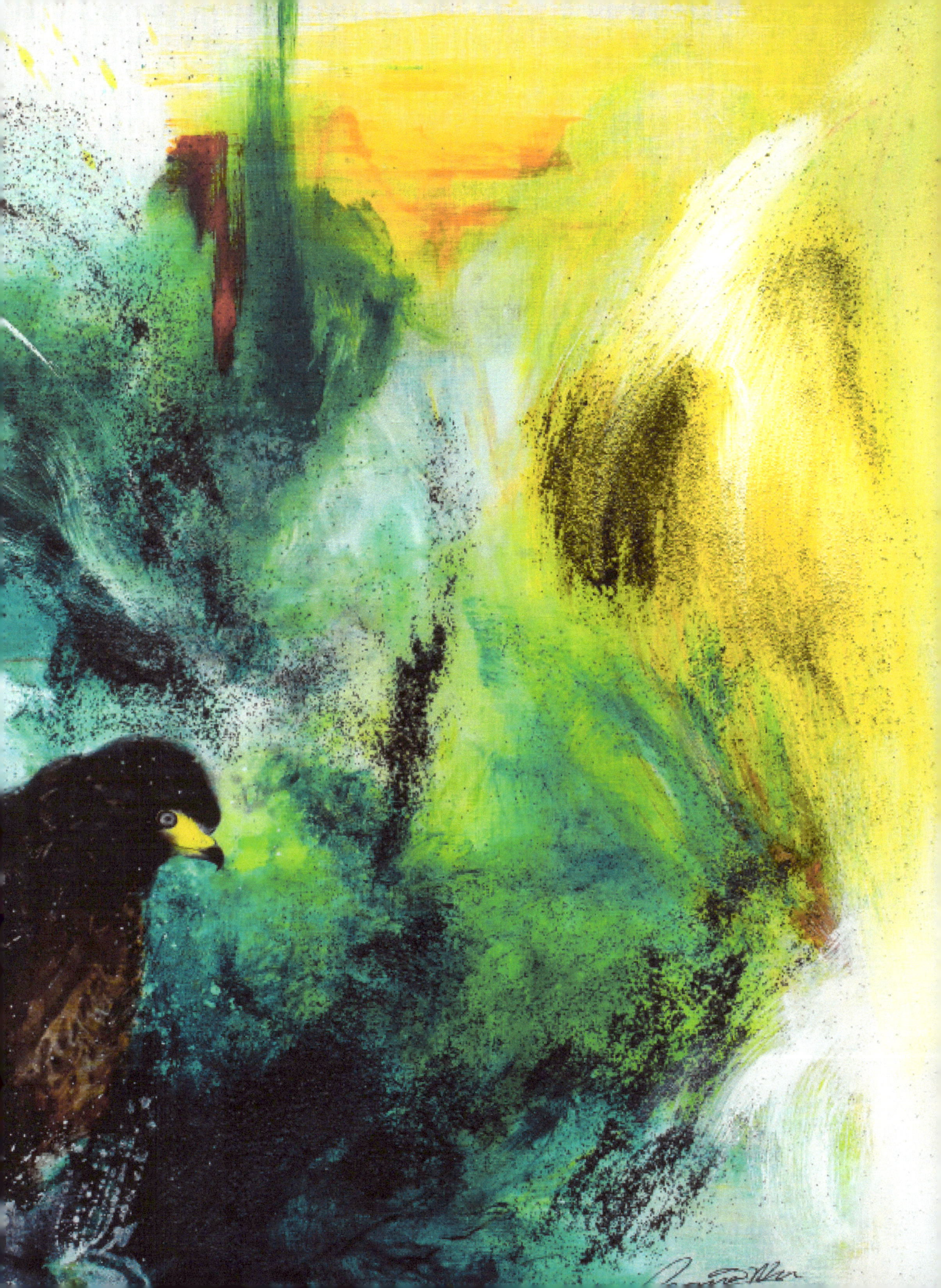

Running Trees Oil on Canvas   78.7"   × 55.1"   2009

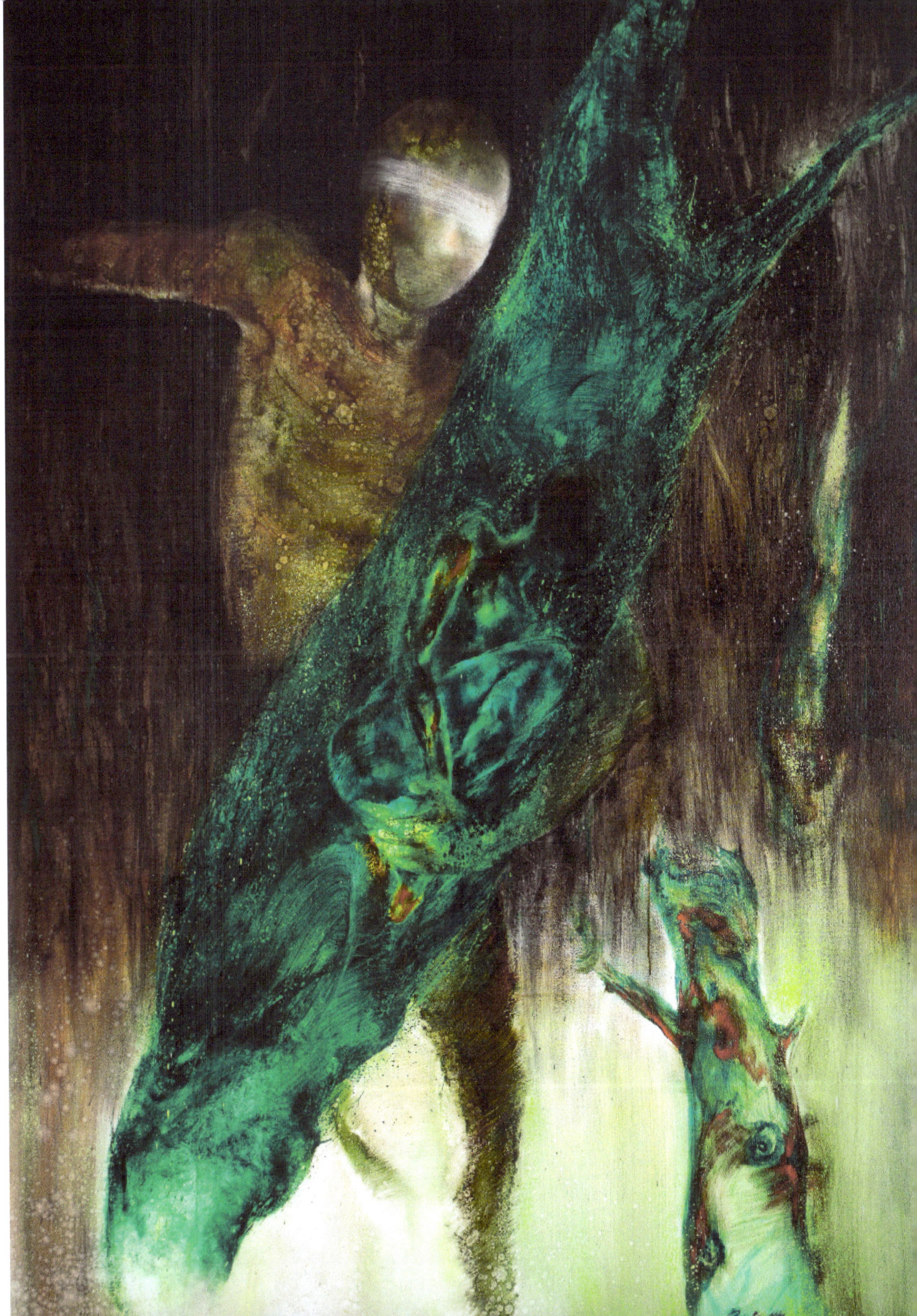

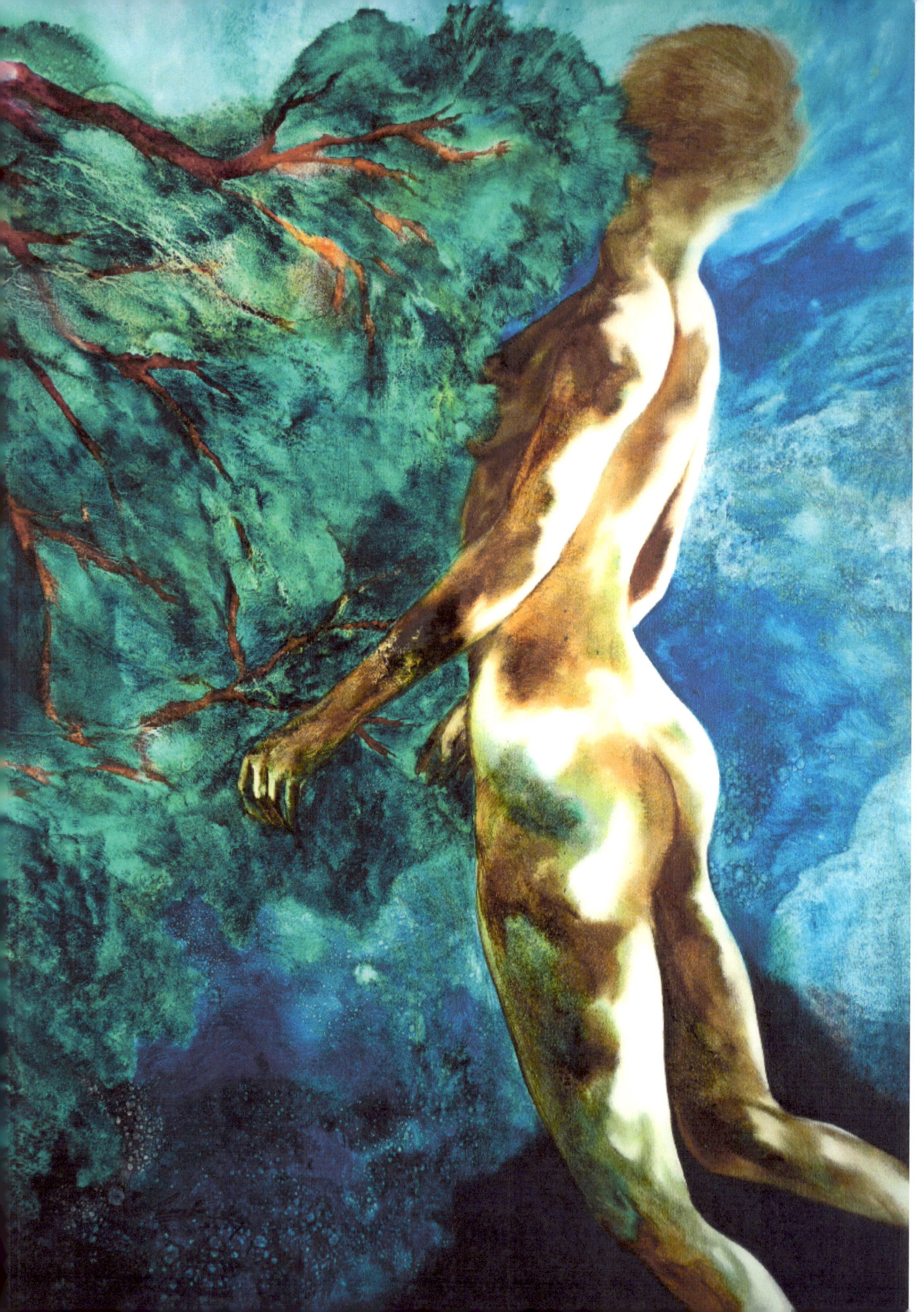

Breathe Oil on Canvas   70.8"   × 55.1"   2009

Memory of the Sea Oil on Canvas   59" × 47.2"   2011

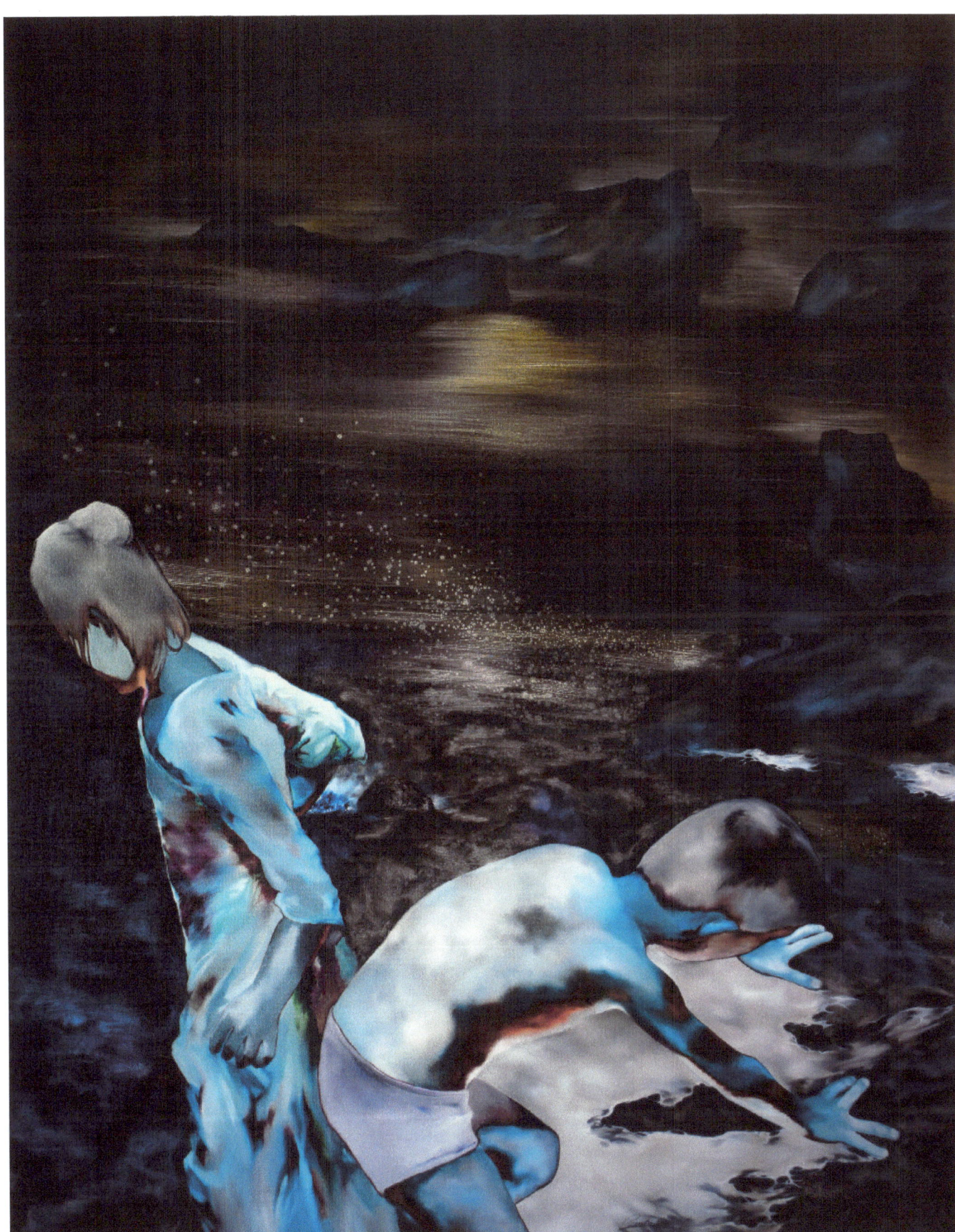

Go Home Oil on Canvas   78.7" × 51.1"   2011

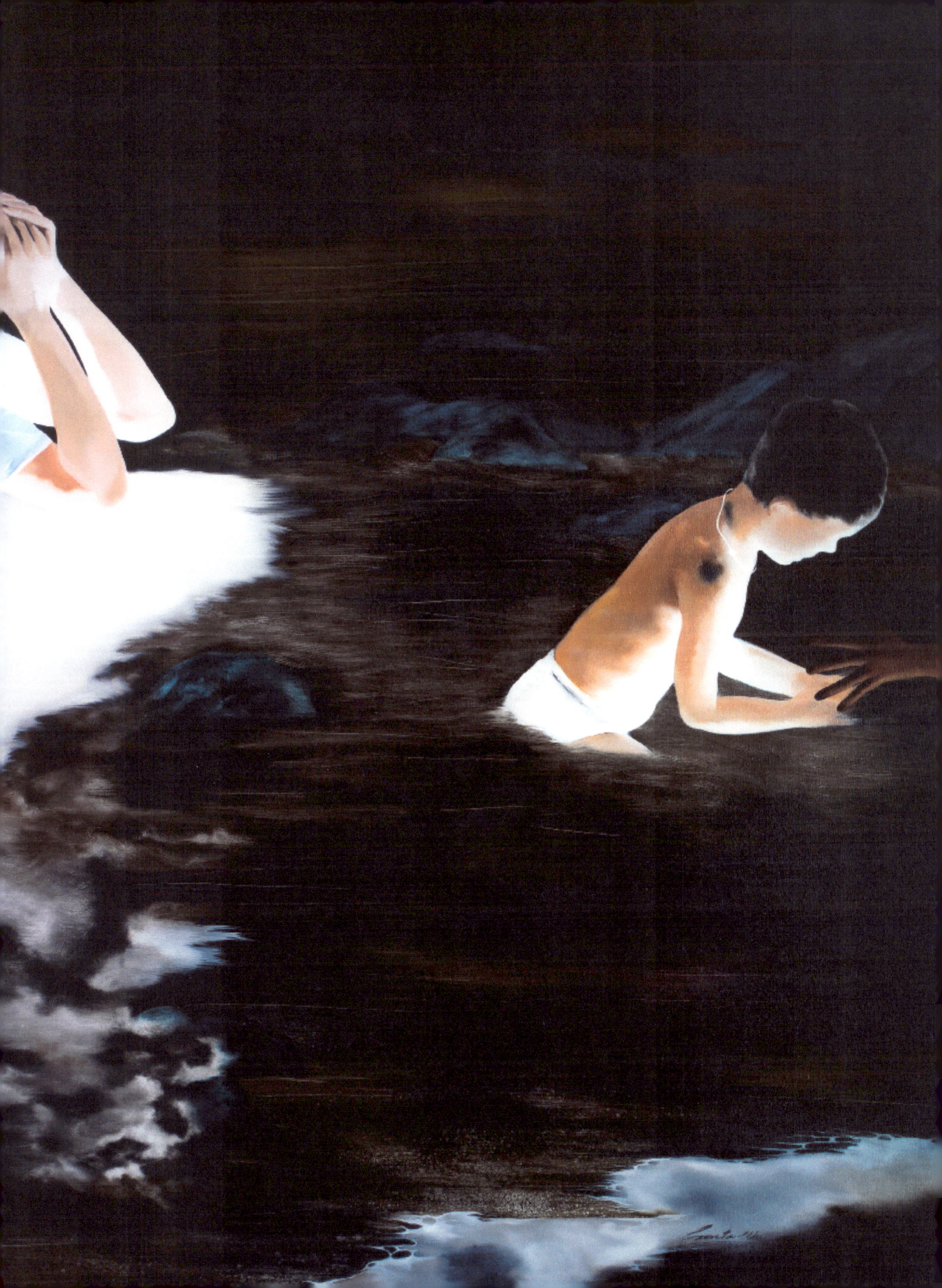

Walk   Oil on Canvas   78.7" × 47.2"   2011

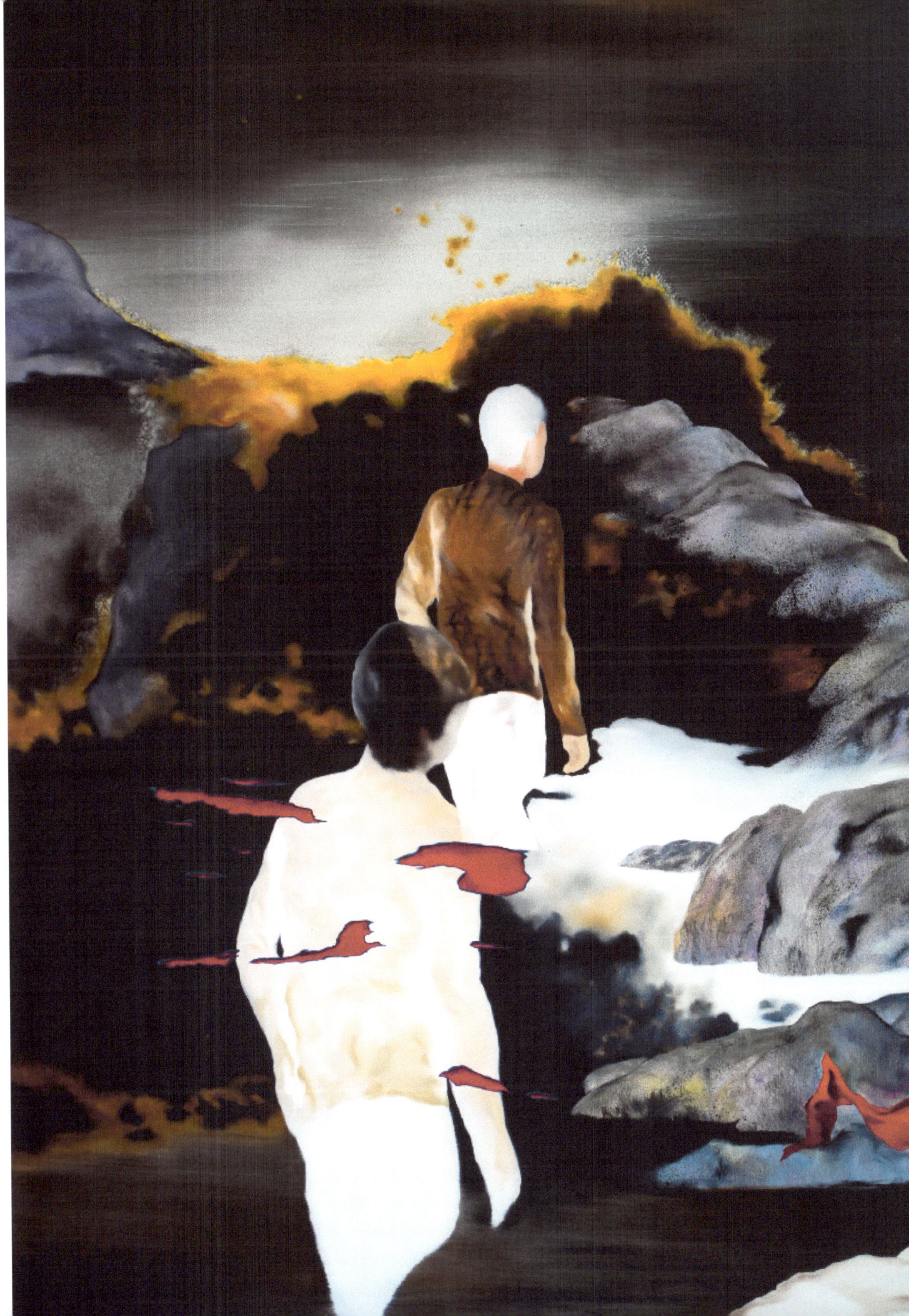

Boys Oil on Canvas　59"　× 59"　2012

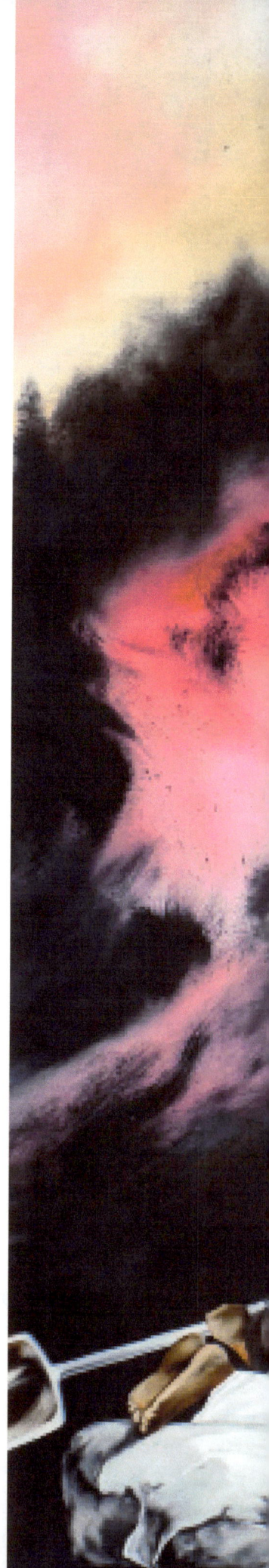

Embarrassing Stay Oil on Canvas　59"　× 78.7"　2012

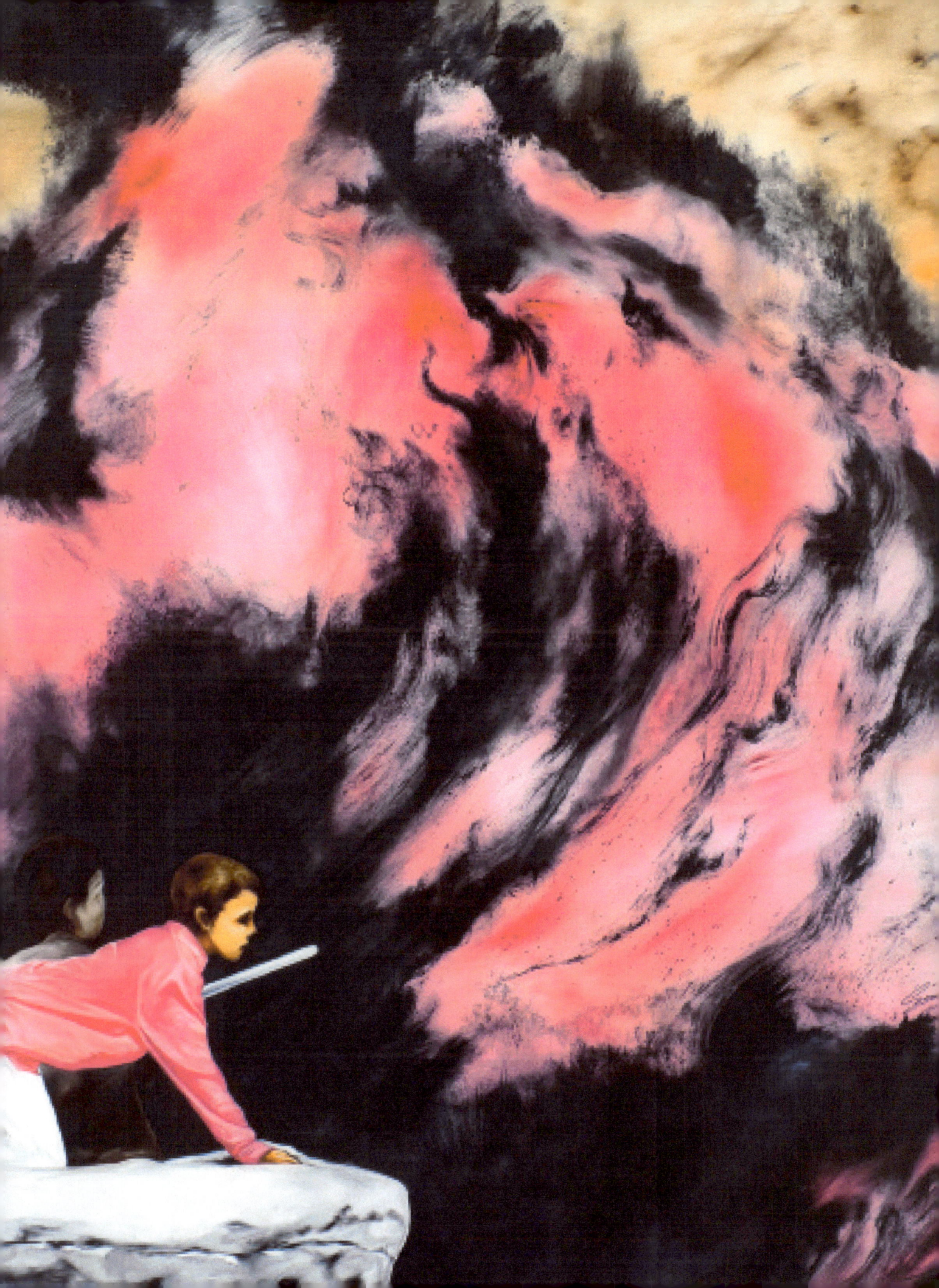

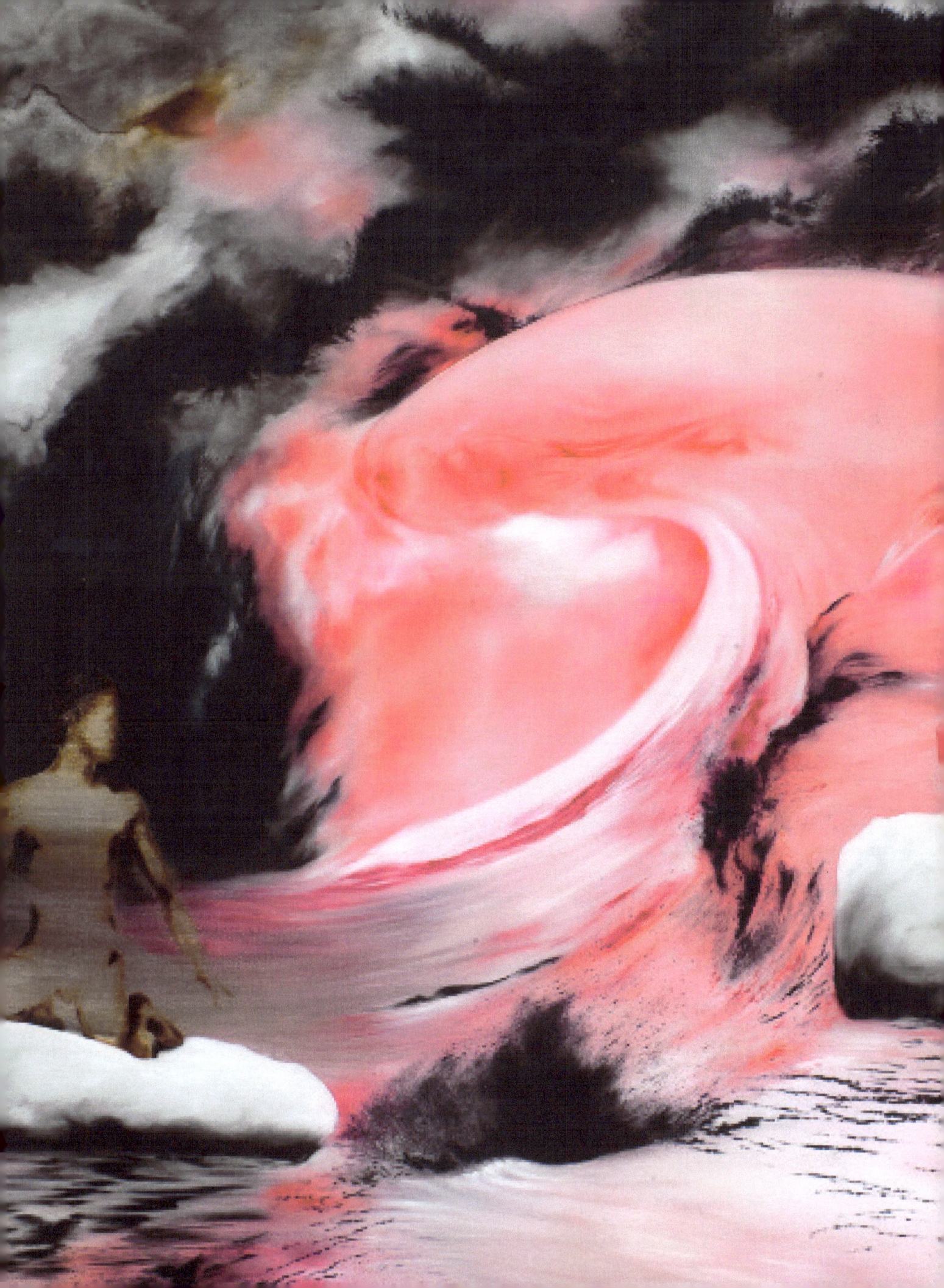

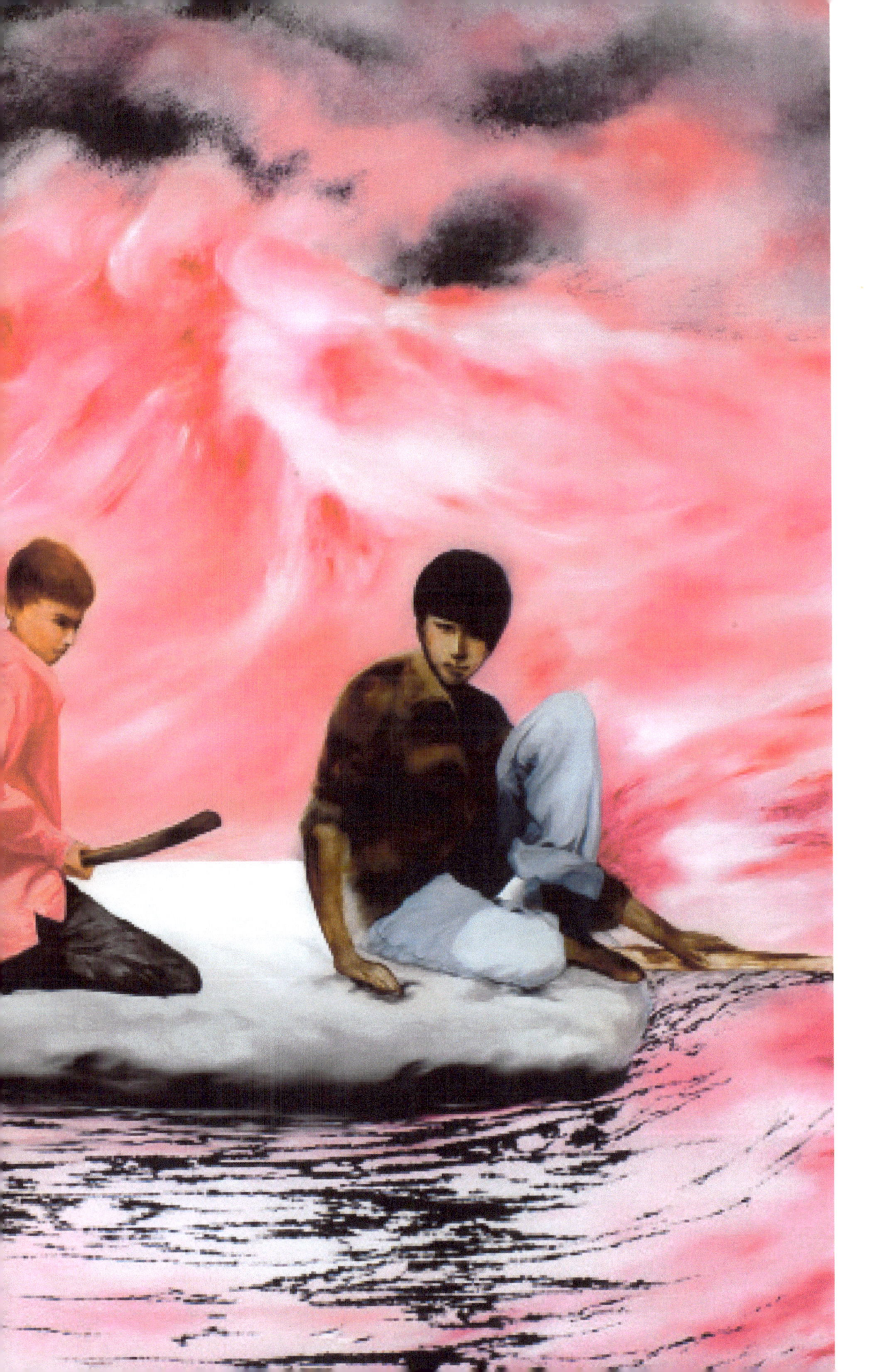

Memory Whirlpool Oil on Canvas   35.4 " × 23.6"   2010

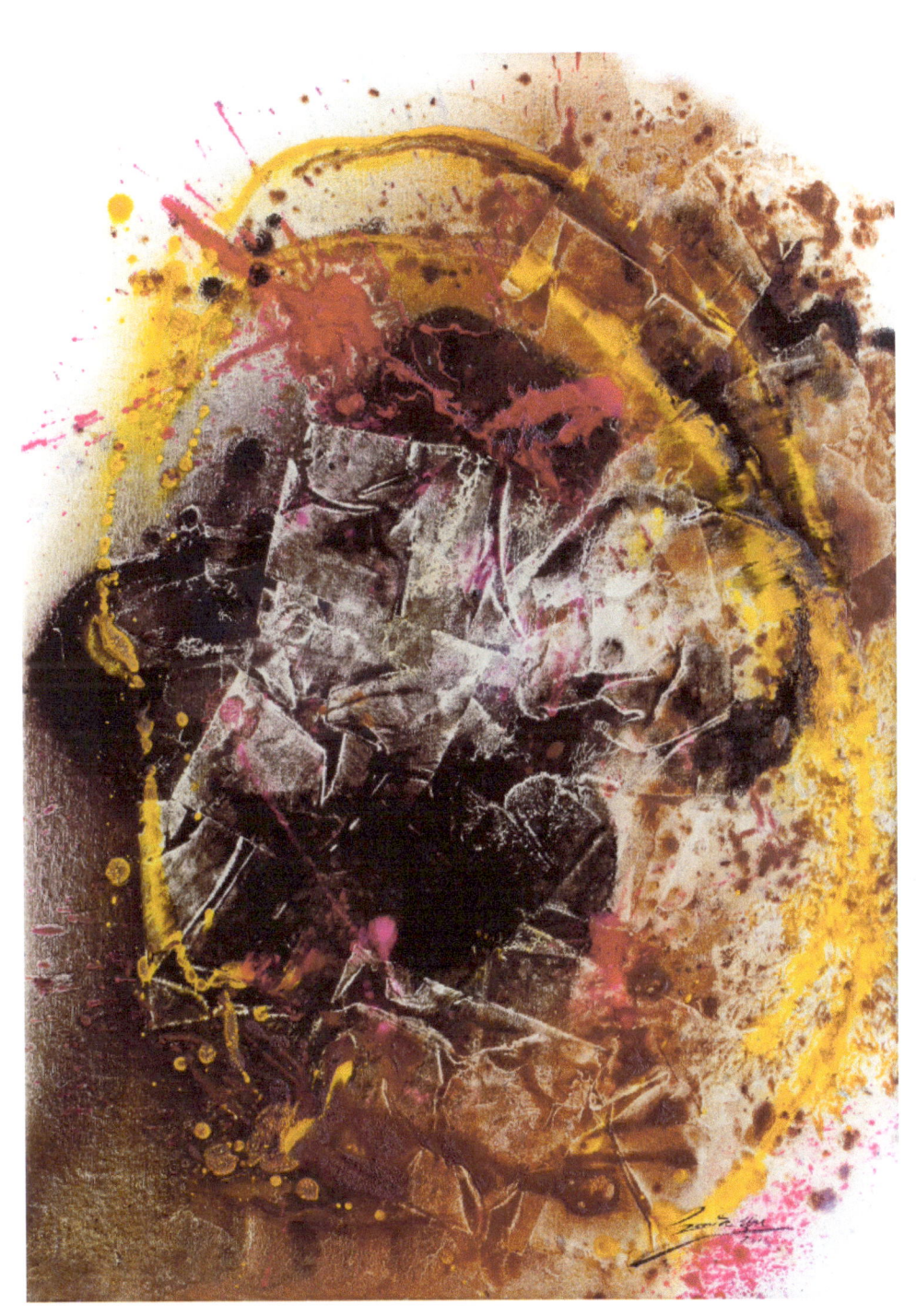

Dream Oil on Canvas   39.4 " × 31.5"   2010

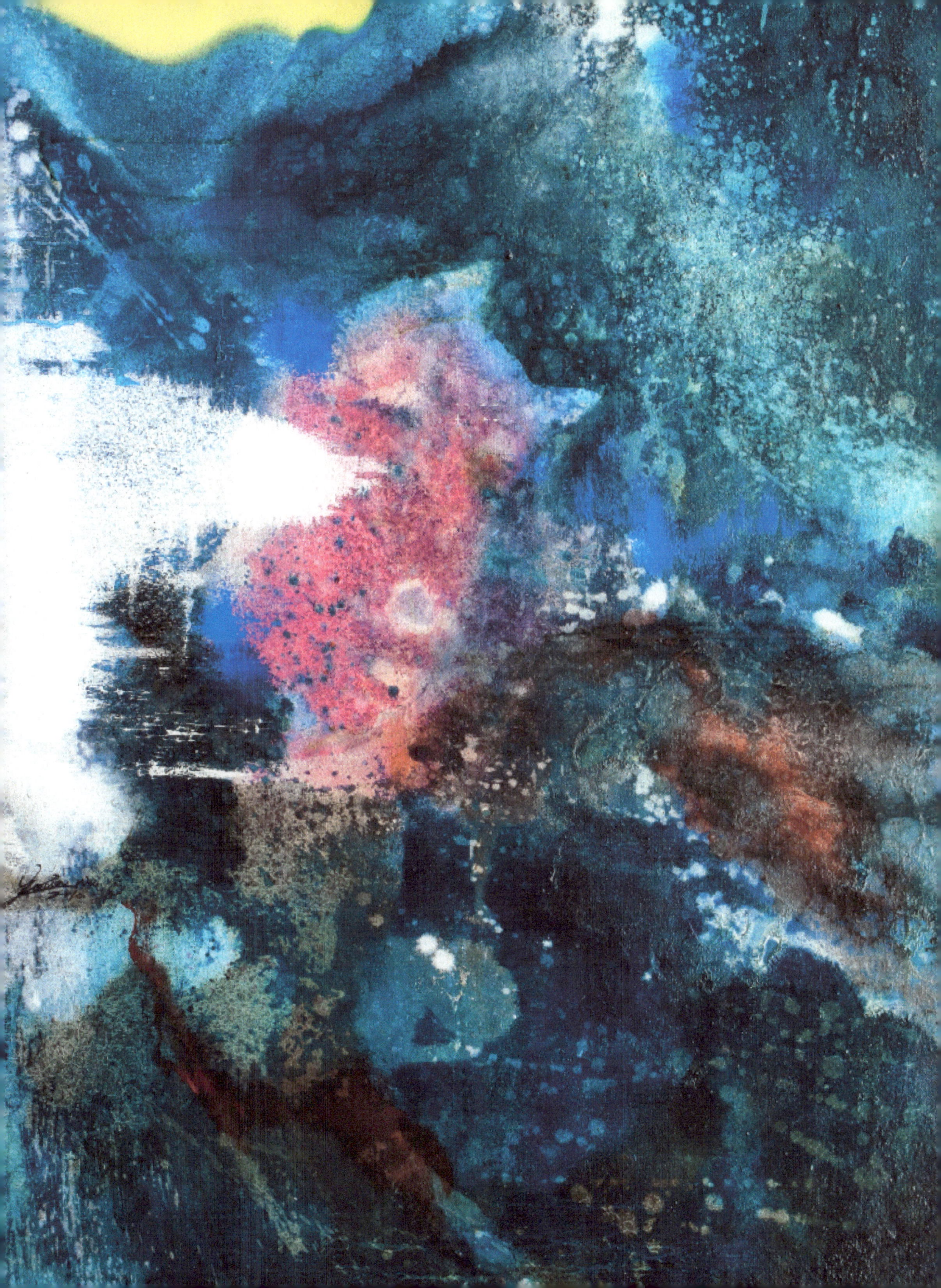

Chiwen Oil on Canvas   70.8"   × 55.1"   2009

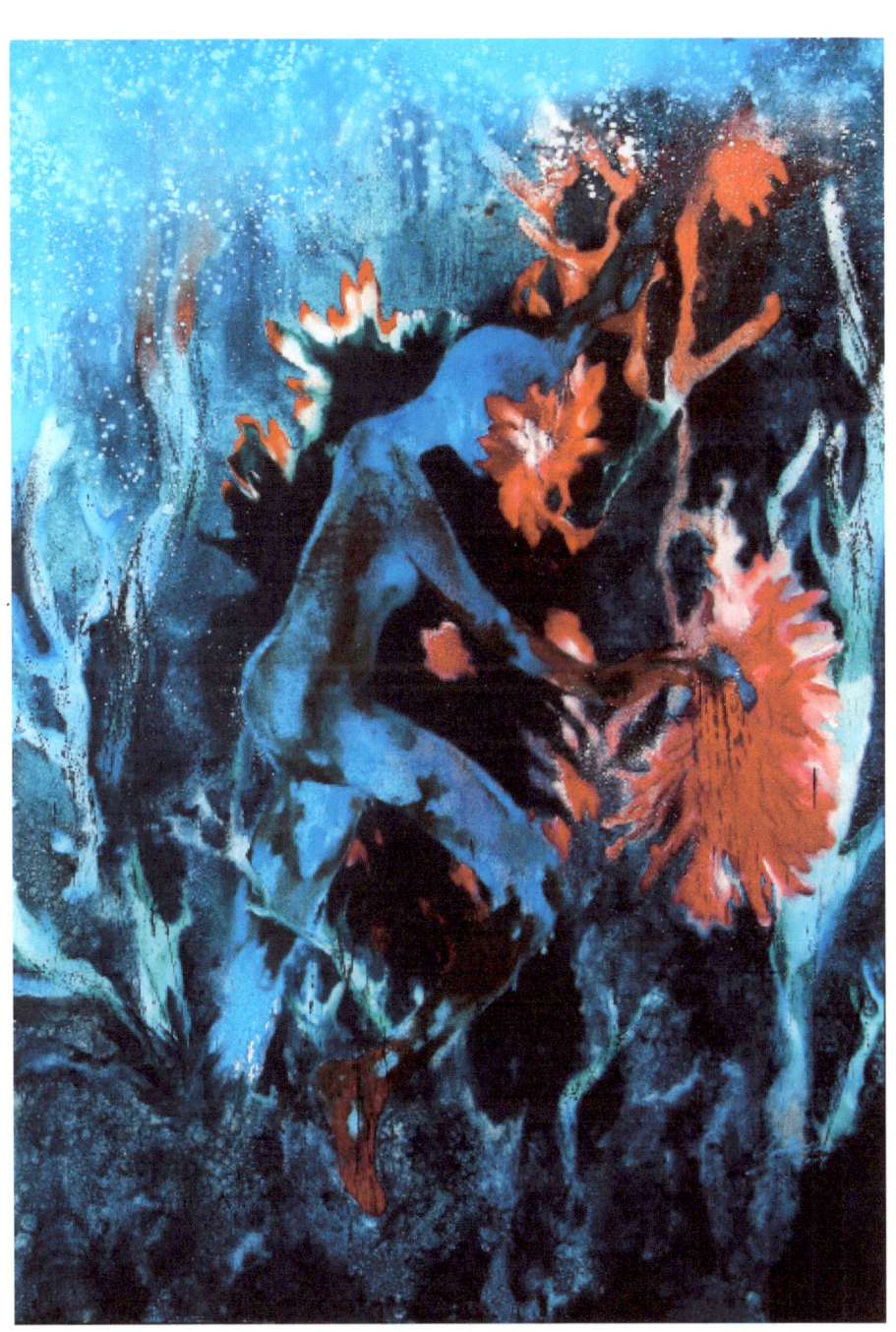

Swam Dance Oil on Canvas   31.5 " × 39.4"   2012

Loneliness Appeal Oil on Canvas   35.4"   × 47.2"   2012

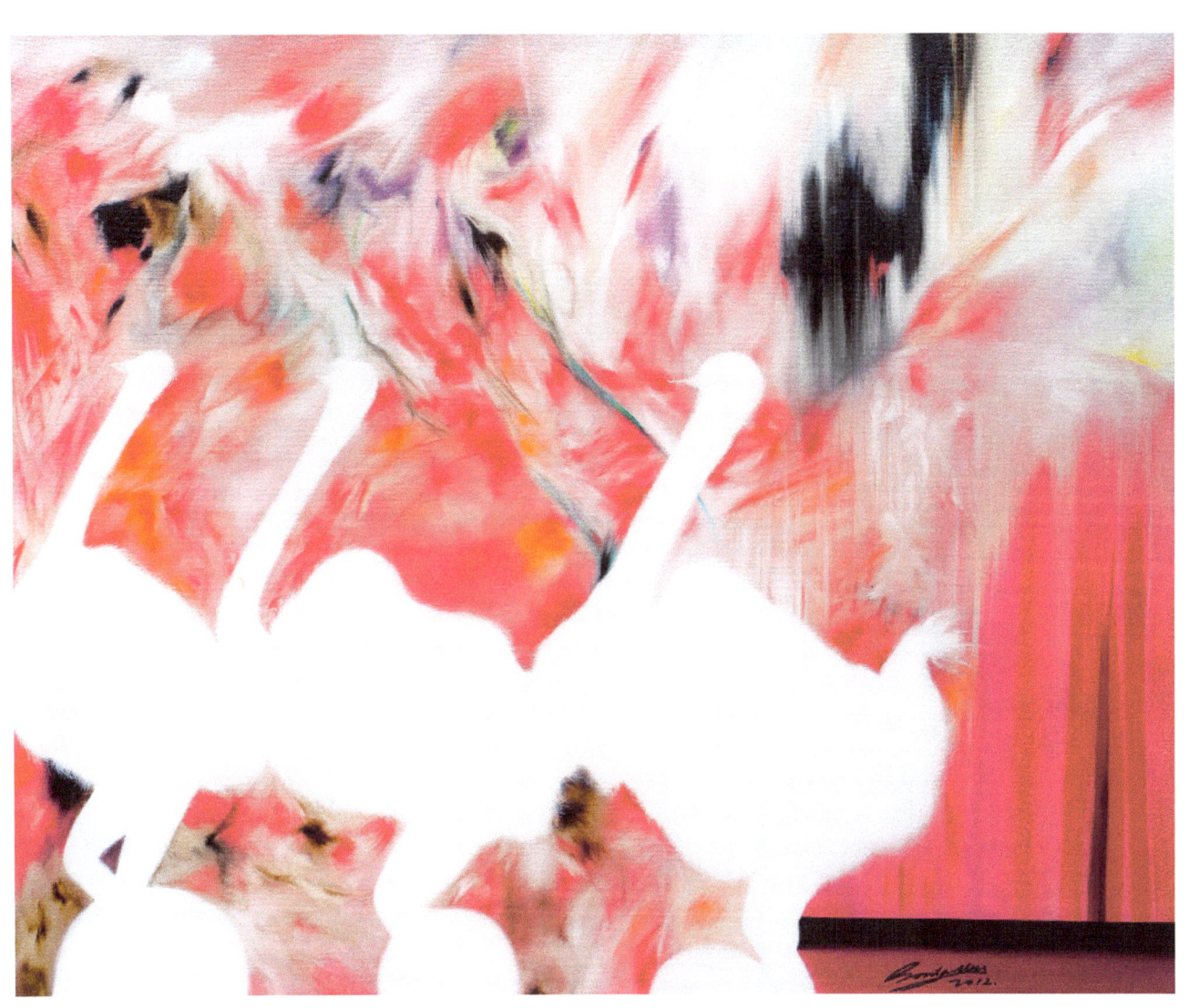

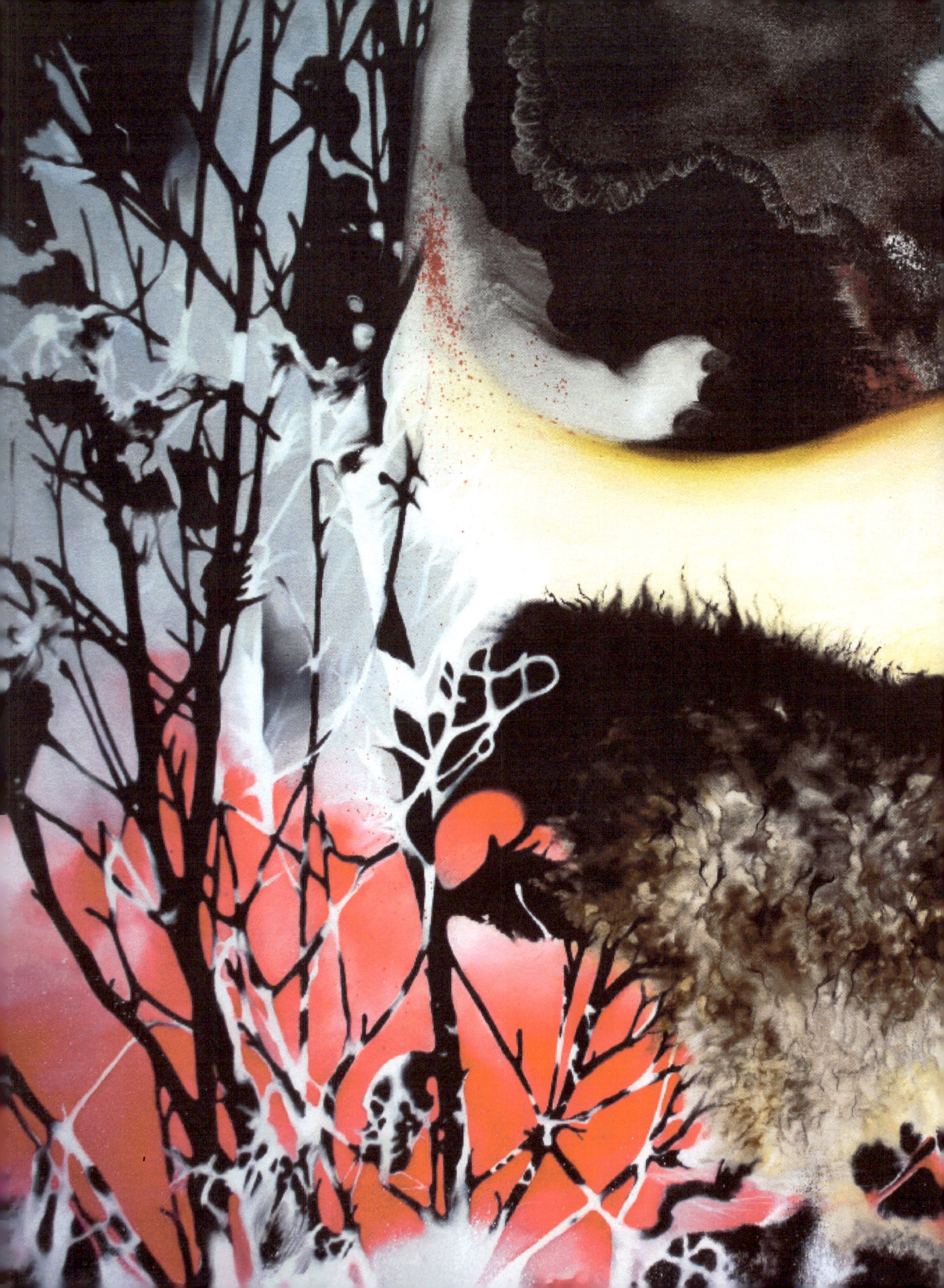

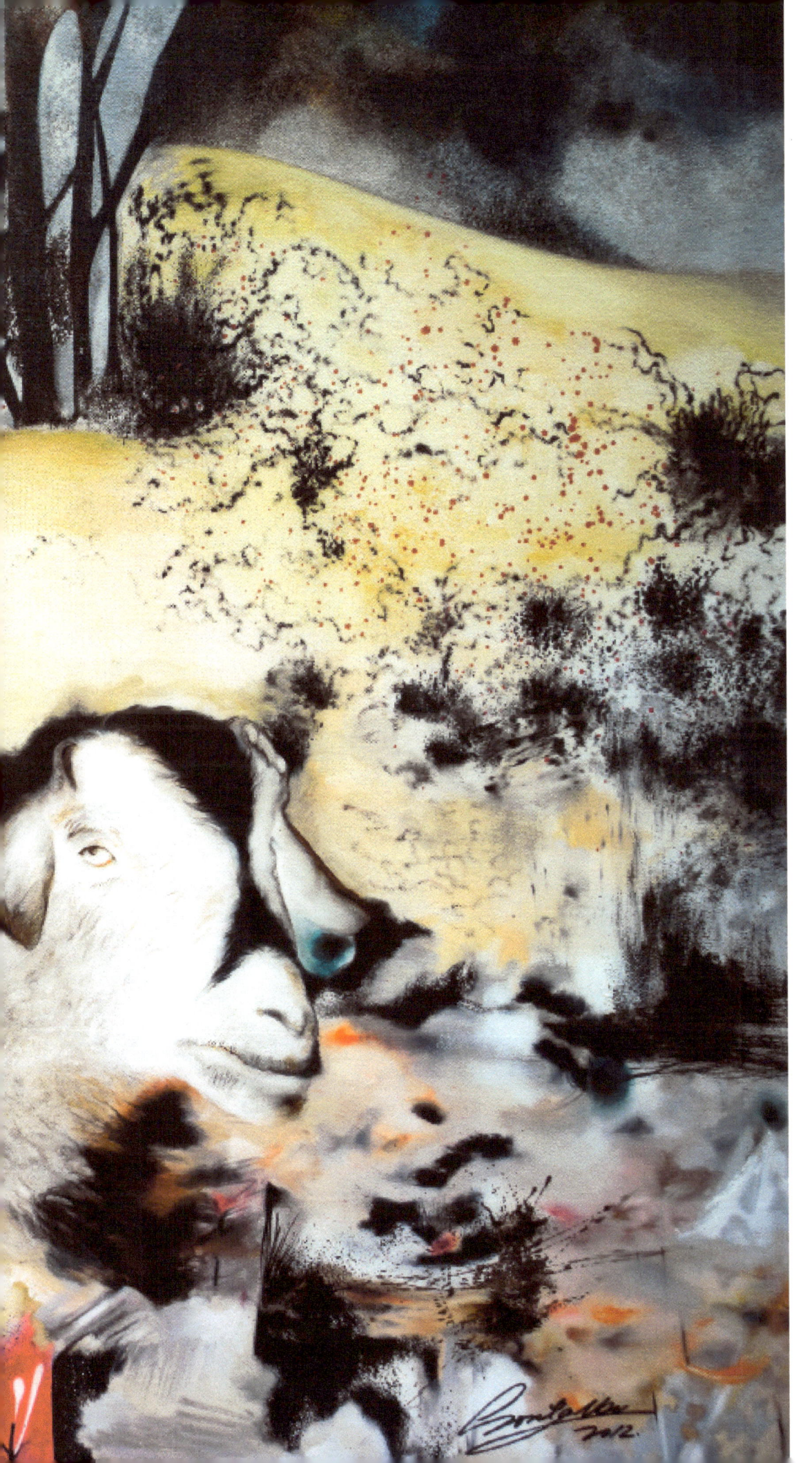

Liberty & Romantic Oil on Canvas   31.5"   × 47.2"   2011

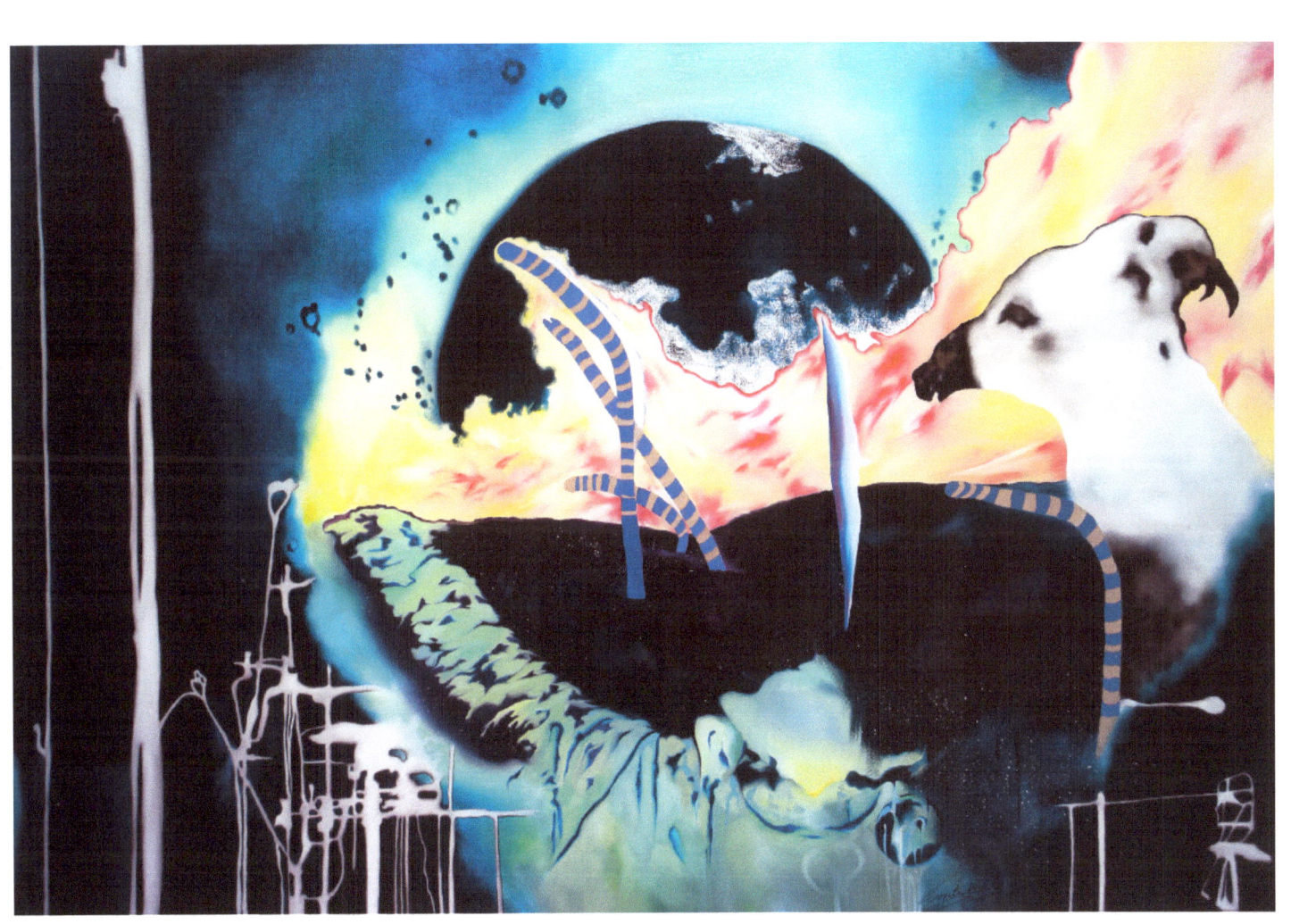

Rambo Oil on Canvas   39.4 " × 31.5"   2012

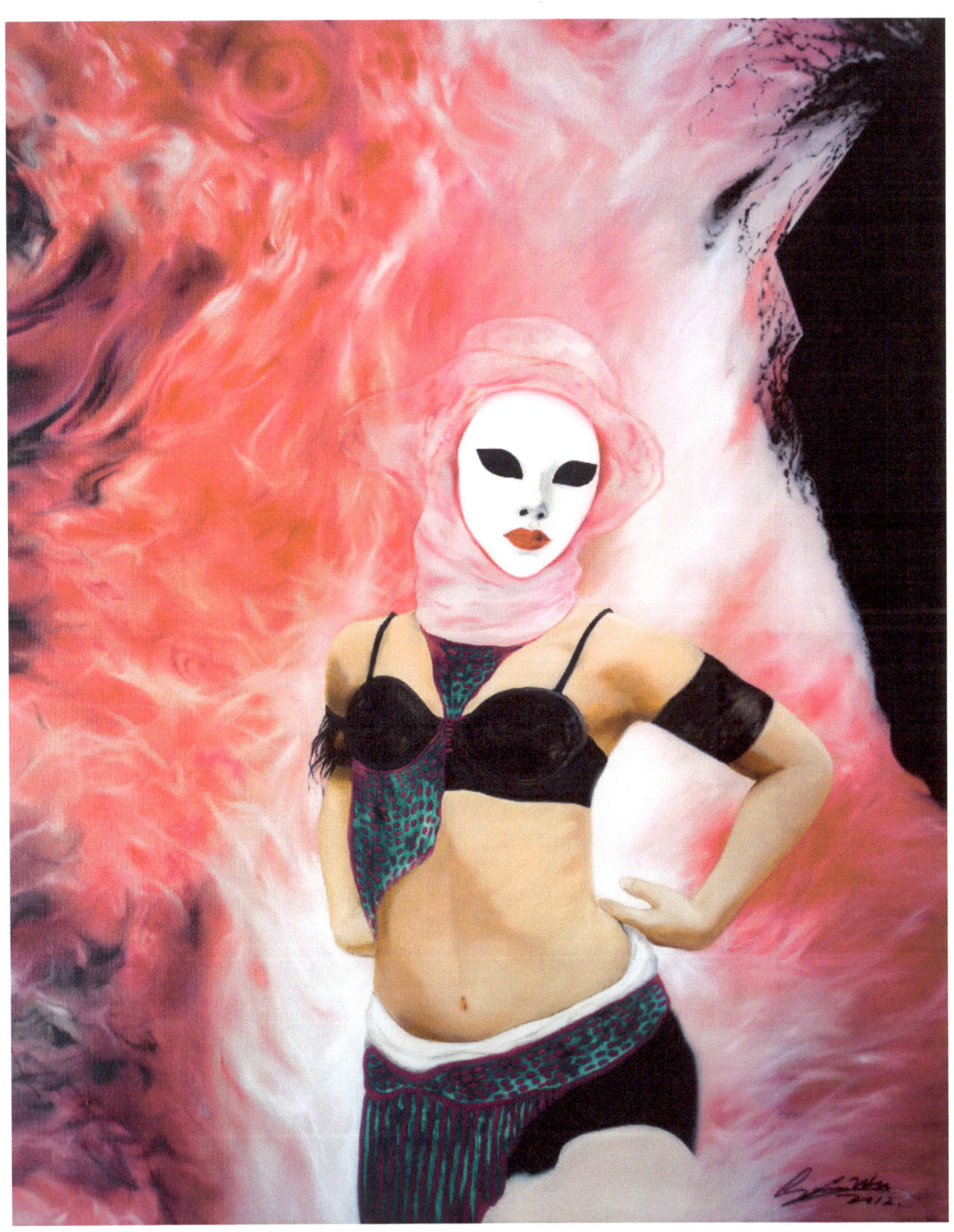

Sunset Oil on Canvas   31.5" × 47.2"   2012

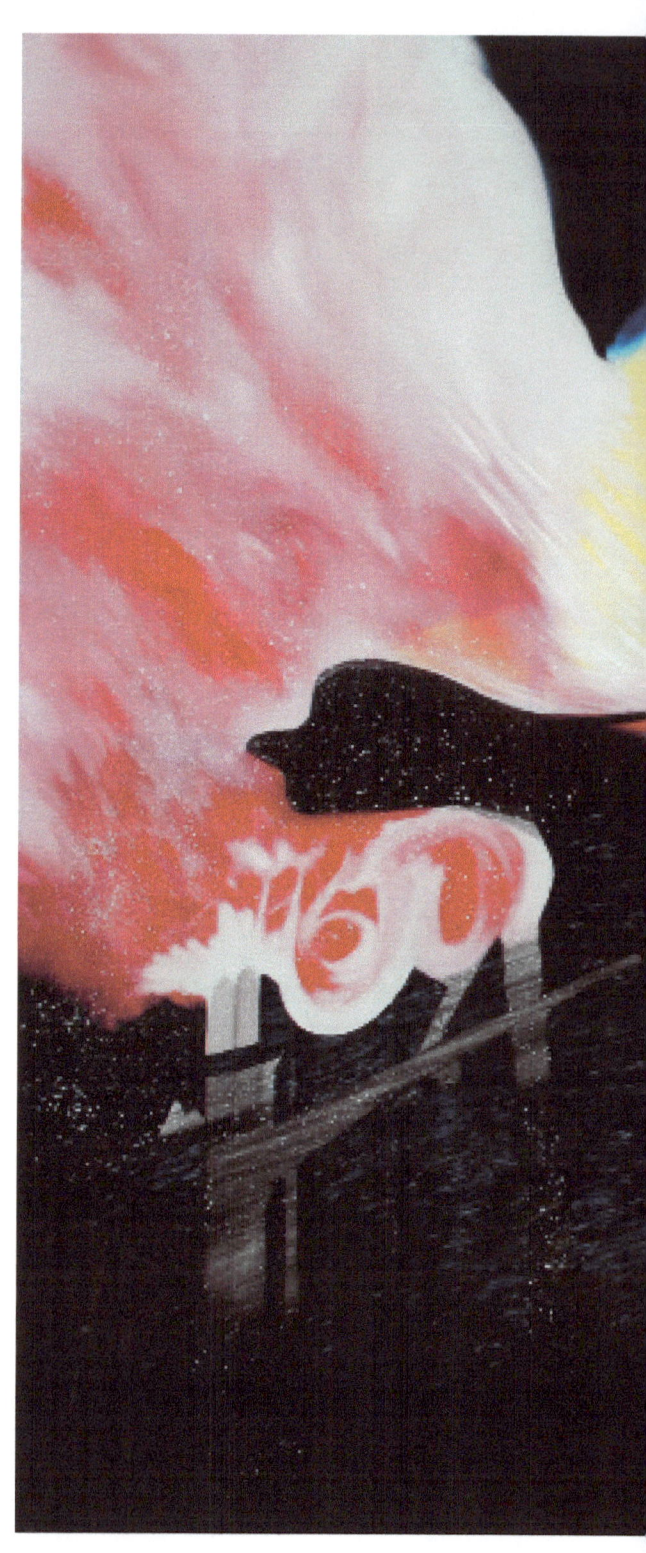

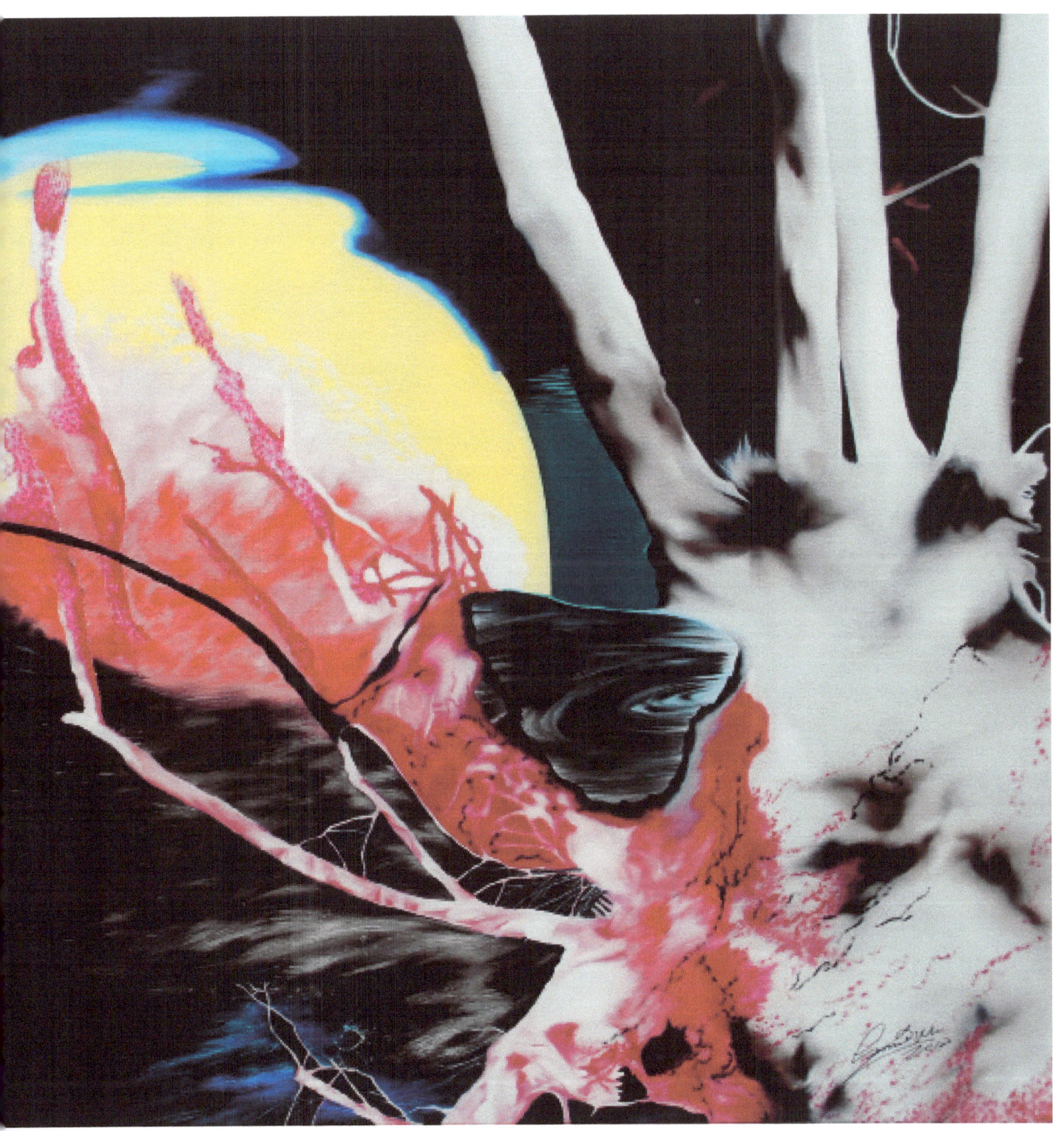

Bride Oil on Canvas 39.7"φ 2014

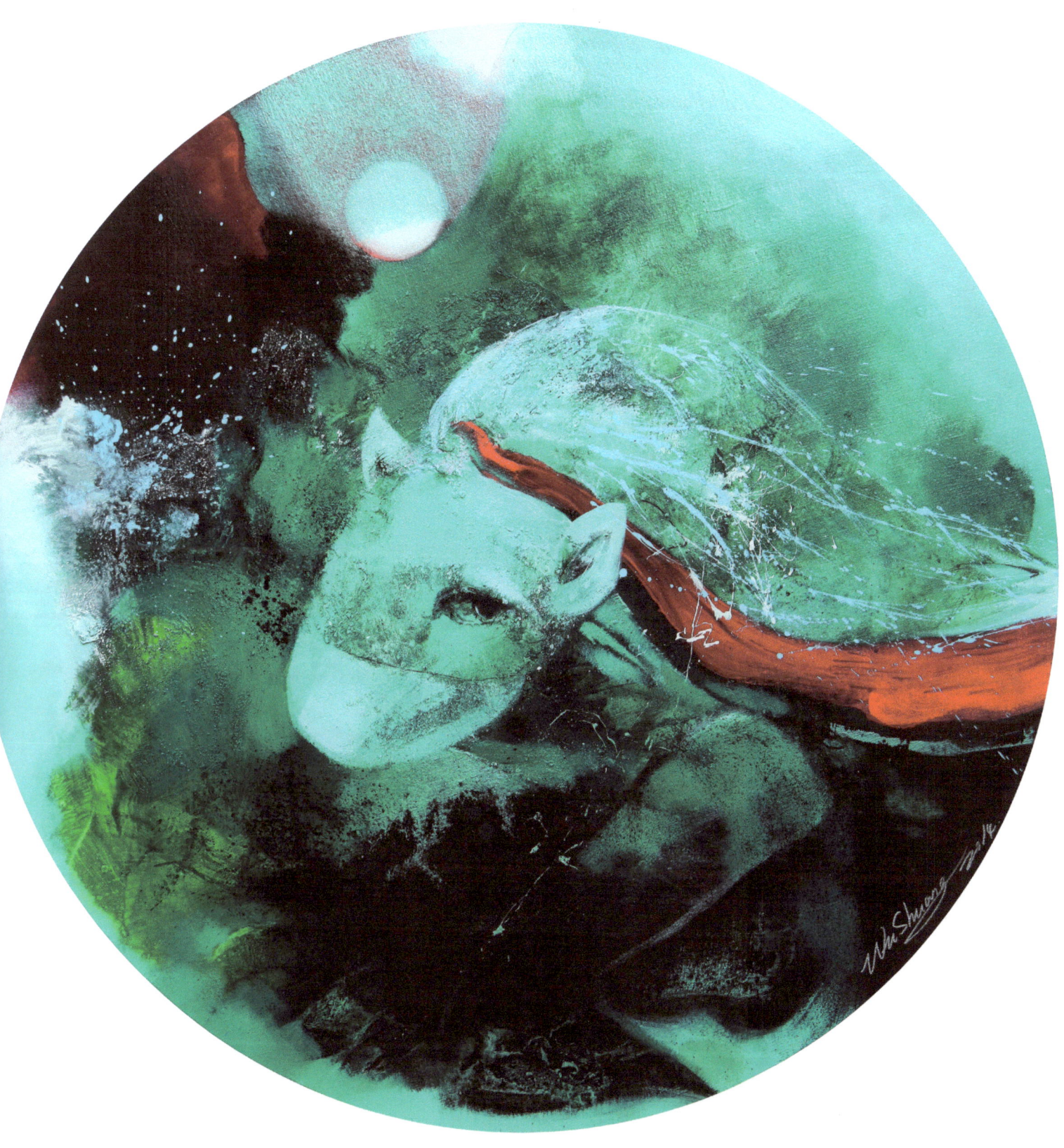

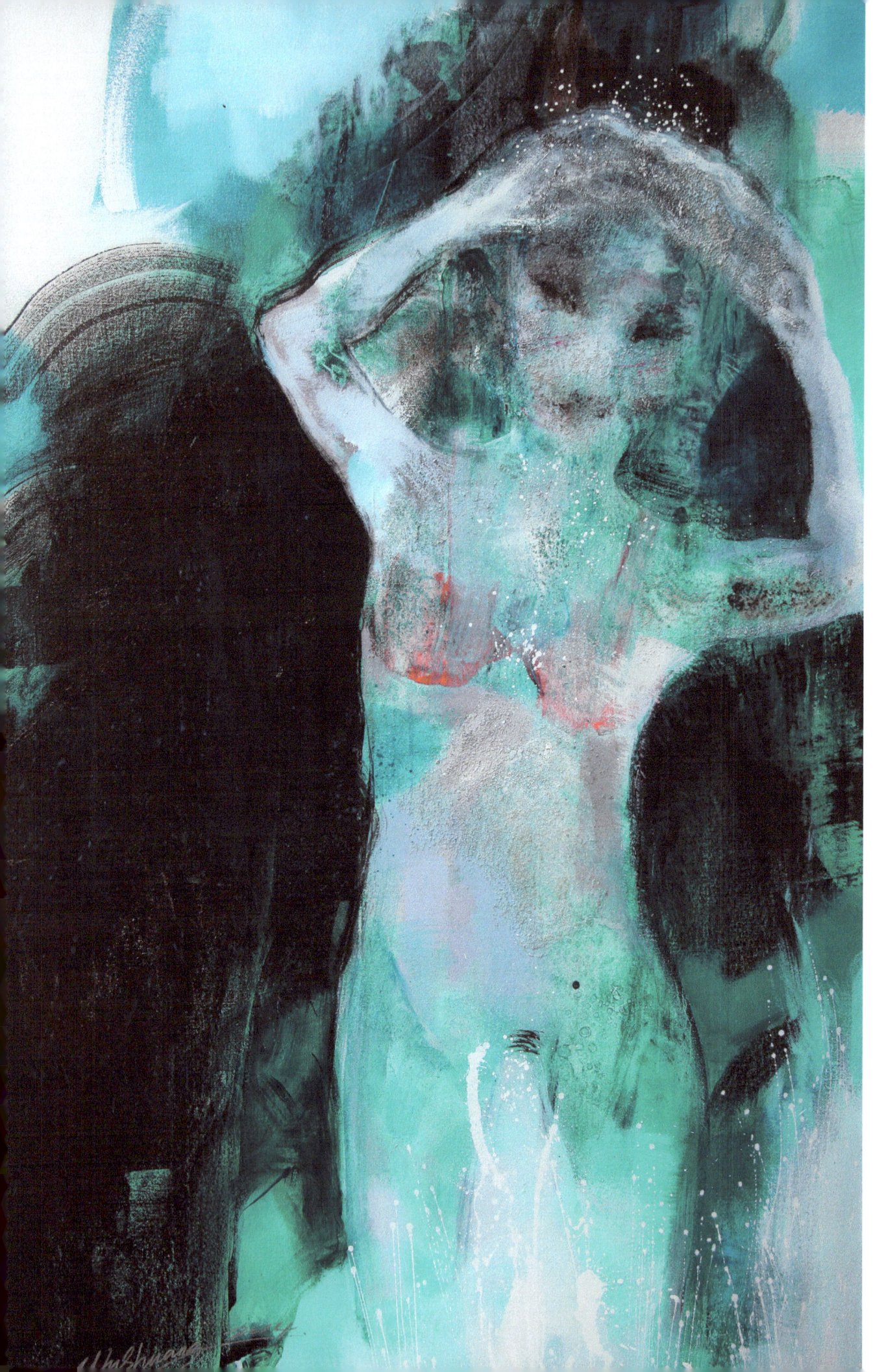

Deny   Oil on Canvas 47.2"   × 31.5"   2014

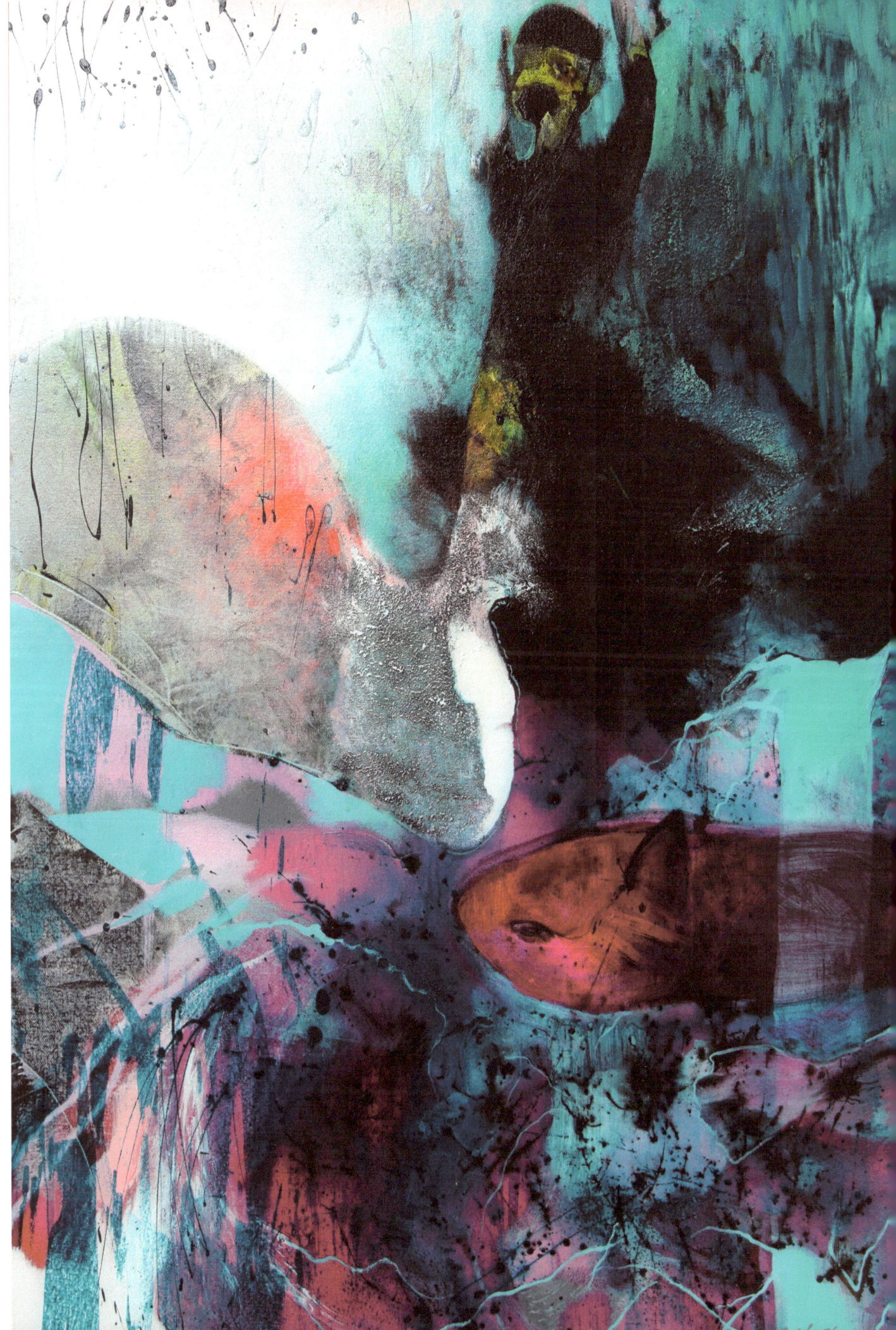

Beauty Oil on Canvas 39.7"φ 2013

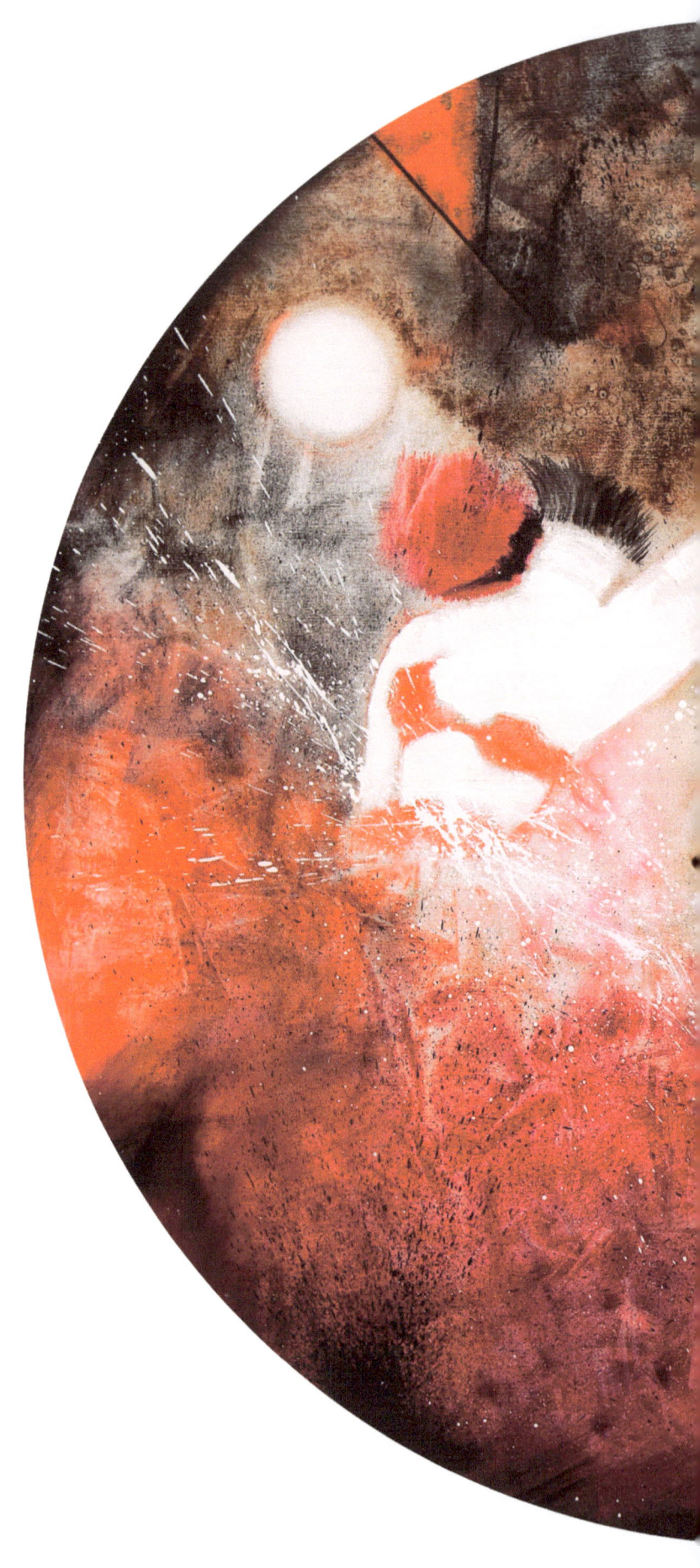

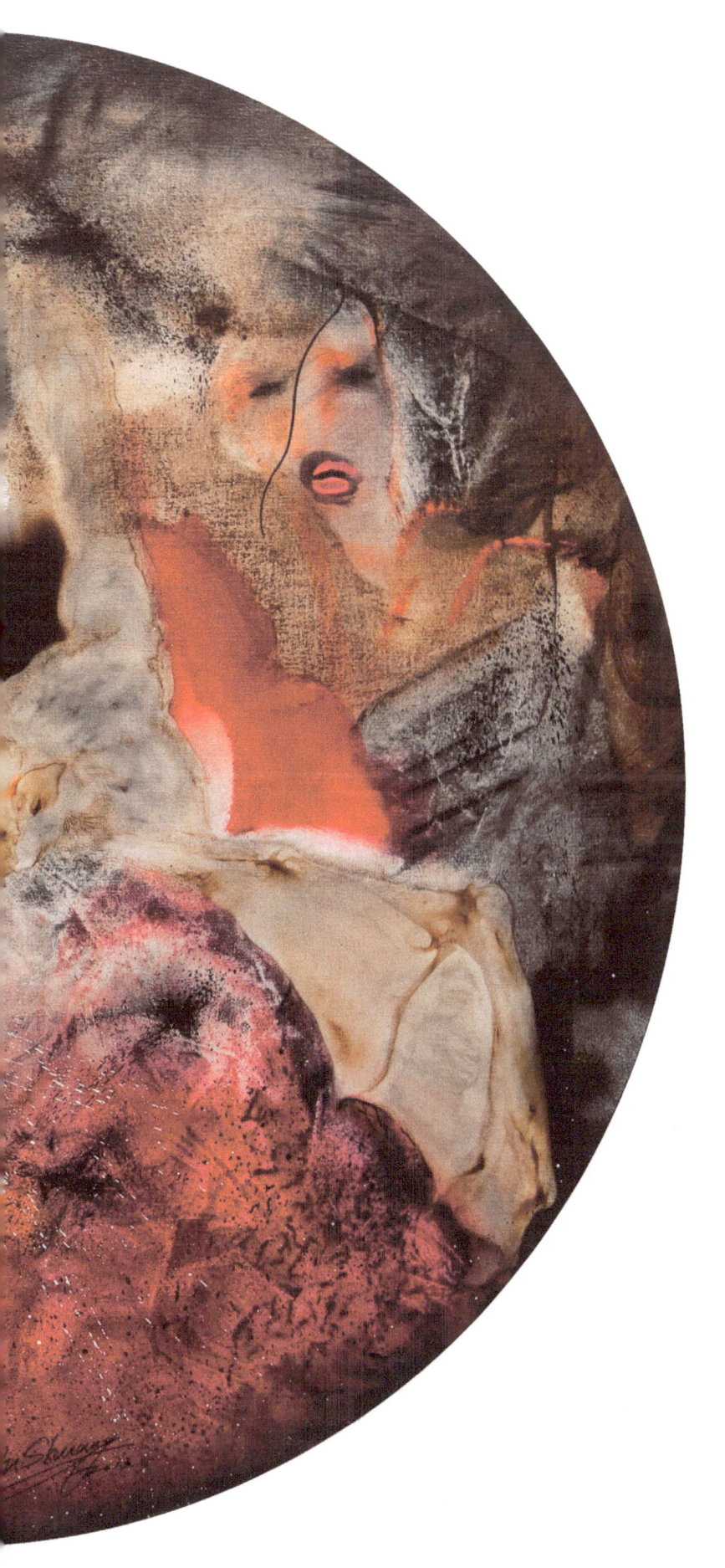

Butterfly Effect Oil on Canvas 78.7" × 189" 2013

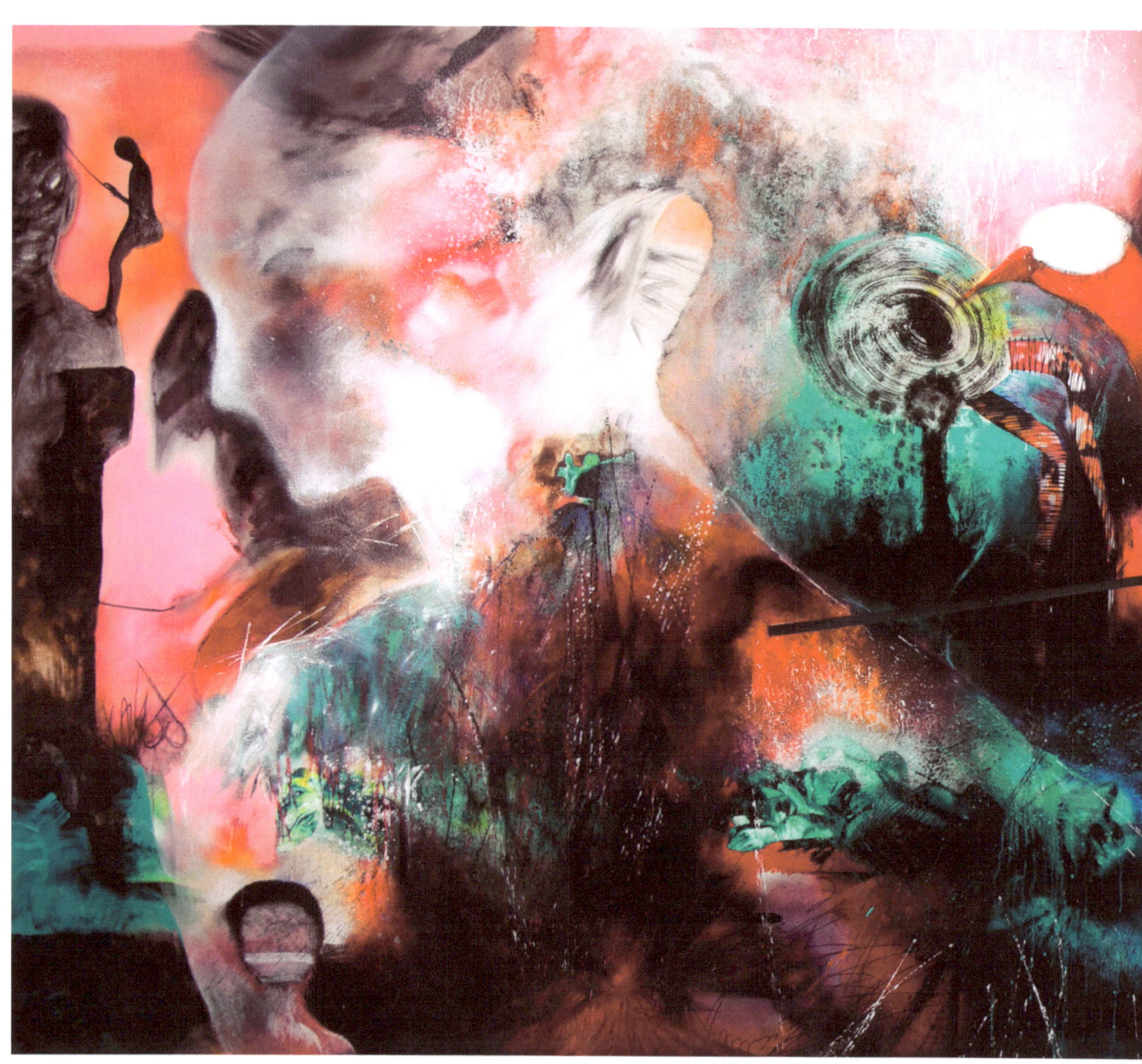

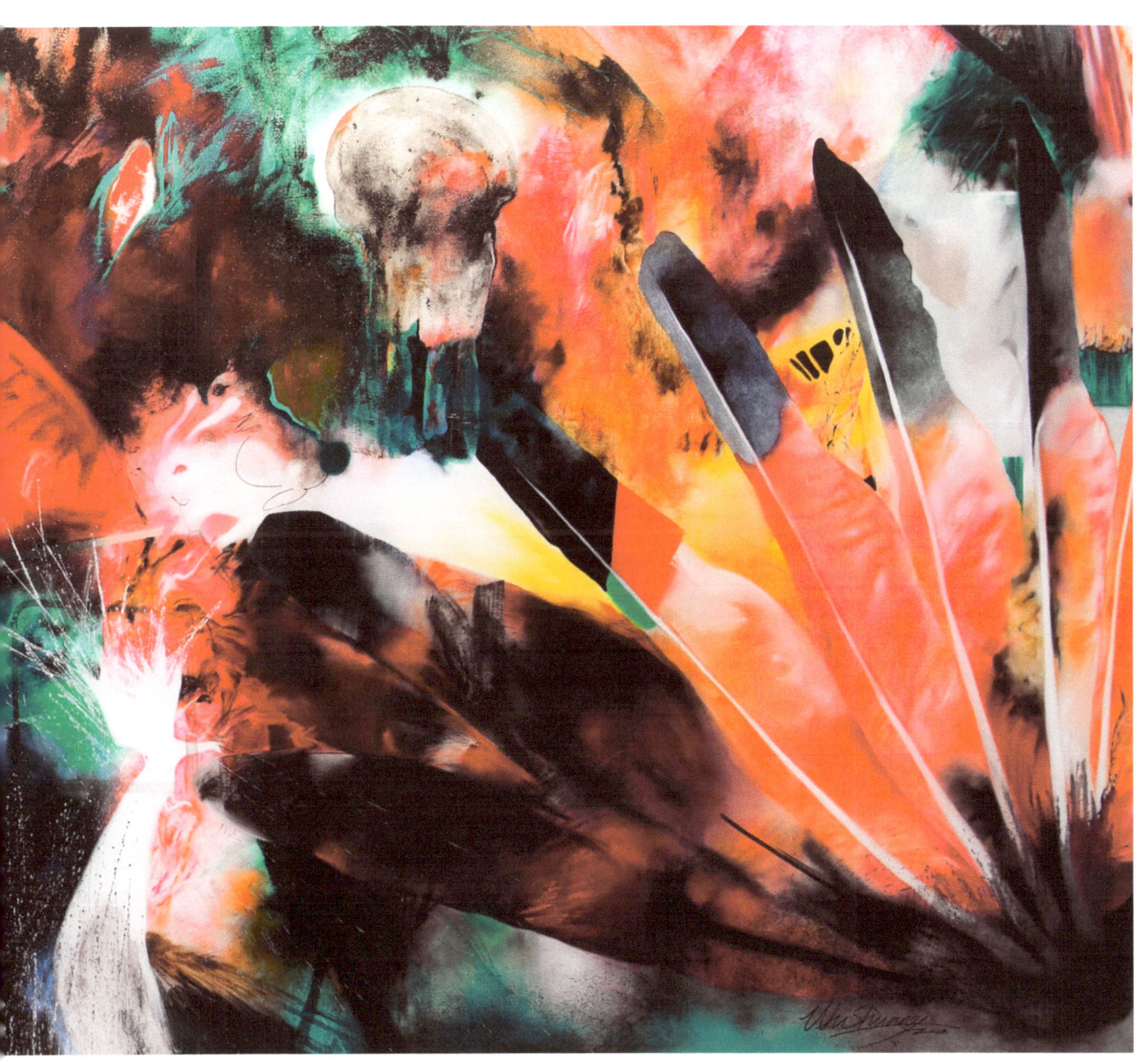

Postscript

She Prefers Observing the Beauty Above
Written by Dong Xiyun

Soul and flesh, dream and reality – make a choice.

This is a world with too many dream pursuers and very few dream catchers. To the latter, the public compliment fades next to what they are doing. They do not care about what their works would end up being even though they create, write and paint like they are supernaturally crazy. It is because they would be drowned as long as they do not swim hard against the waves, not to mention swim overwhelmingly forward.

Painting is as important to Wu Shuang as swimming is to a drowning man.

It was a wine party where I met her for the very first time. It was an all-girl party with many girls and very little wine. I laid my eyes on a girl with big boobs and slim waist when everybody was chatting. She did neither eat foods nor drink wine. It occurred to me that the quiet girl who sat across me can be as shrewish as water spinach to be going into boiling oil as I spent more time with her. She was crisp and straightforward like she will always be.

I got drunk when I met her again. She insisted driving me home. I could not remember what she said in the car. The only thing left in my mind is that I looked her up and down repeatedly while wondering why she still looks very pretty without make-up. It would be the best if I were a man. Or, it is also fine to me so long as cocks grow all over me.

Oriana Fallaci remarked that this is a man-for-man world and women are created to please men and bring them troubles. Obviously, the rule does not work for Wu Shuang. She never dubbed herself a feminist or a moral pioneer. "It is very painstaking to be a woman. I will be definitely devoted to the cause of feminism!" she said while grabbing hold of my hand after we had a long talk.

I would also see her painting when i was not knocking over a drink. She stands there on the painting ladder with half a foot off ground. The painting brush in her hand moves dazzlingly as if it was flowing liquid. Dish-sized gorgeous flowers are blossoming one after another as she moves the painting brush, creating eternal masterpieces like the pyramid under the moonlight.

"Boys" is my favorite. The two exquisite-looking boys are bending on the sailboard with the pink high tides going to swallow them from their back. The black warm current just sits next to them. Like two slices of velvet floating amid the flood, they look young, fine and vulnerable. This is a great height of supreme perfection that not everyone would reach only with weeks or months of efforts.

"Beauty" . The climax of beauty is located at "combined appreciation of elegance and popularity" . Wu Shuang's works represent a perfect combination of "beauty of heaven or soul" and "beauty sensed in real life" . Her works are absolutely not all about "obscurity" like they seem. It is because she sometimes intends to convey to people a delicate, exquisite and highly-spiritual "elegance" that comes from her inner world. However, some of her works are only about her dialogue with her inner beast. Full of originality and ingenuity, her works are like a piece of frozen music or a love letter, or more like a mature girl's body shedding brilliance, which presents an idea that you do not have to face death in the end of life even though you have been through a painful childhood.

To her "She gets incased in whoever she must be. She gets the way to freedom only when she gets rid of who she must be" .

She prefers observing above to enjoy the moon's beauty but something on the ground.

Apr.2013 Chongqing

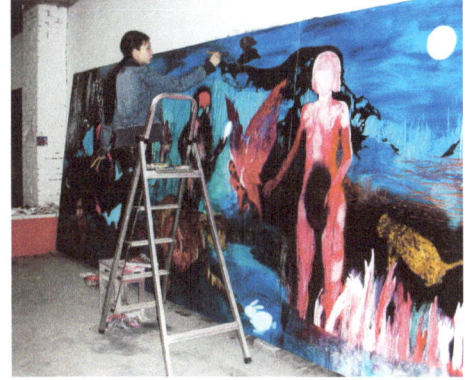

Presented:Sonia S.Wu Art Studio

Book(Album) Title
The unique paintings of Sonia S. Wu: A modern female artist living in Beijing (1)
Artist: Sonia Shuang Wu
Created and Editor: S. Sherman Zhang

Studio: Zone A, Huantie International Art Center, Beijing, China
E-mail: wushuangart@foxmail.com

Art Design: Xue Siruo

Chinese Proofreading: Dong Xiyun

English Proofreading: Wei Liming

Translation: Ma Dan

Photograph: Cheng Yizhong

Copywriter: Wang Xiaojian   Liu Zhehan   Yu Haisheng
Liang Yuan   Dong Xiyun